"When I am at the farm, I often follow my network of trails
through the woods, across the prairie, along the flats and down
the hills and around the many twists and turns. A trail is not
for hurrying. Despite how familiar the trail is to me now, there
is always something new to see or hear as I wind my way
along. And there are the old friends: a deer bounding in front of
me, the giant oak trees that I dearly love, the views across my
ponds, where I often spot a mallard or a wood duck or a family
of Canada geese. As the seasons change, the views from the
trails change too, from the budding of the trees and the greening
of the grass in spring to the rainbow of colors in fall to the
naked maples in winter. Small side trails here and there lead to
special views: a close-up look at the ponds; a trip to the prairie
restoration. These trails provide access to a vast cross-section of
central Wisconsin nature and landscapes, from upland forestland
to wetlands to prairie. Traveling my farm's nature trails is one of
the great joys of life at Roshara."

Whispers and Shadows: A Naturalist's Memoir

A companion to the
Wisconsin Public Television documentary
THE LAND WITH JERRY APPS

WHISPERS and SHADOWS

We can never have enough of nature.

HENRY DAVID THOREAU

WHISPERS and SHADOWS

A Naturalist's Memoir

Jerry Apps

Wisconsin Historical Society Press

Published by the Wisconsin Historical Society Press
Publishers since 1855

© 2015 by Jerold W. Apps

Publication of this book was made possible in part by a grant from the
D. C. Everest fellowship fund.

For permission to reuse material from *Whispers and Shadows* (ISBN 978-0-87020-709-9; e-book ISBN 978-0-87020-710-5), please access www.copyright.com or contact the Copyright Clearance Center, Inc. (CCC), 222 Rosewood Drive, Danvers, MA 01923, 978-750-8400. CCC is a not-for-profit organization that provides licenses and registration for a variety of users.

wisconsin**history**.org

Printed in Canada
Cover linoleum print © 2015 by John Zimm
Design and cover illustration color by Nancy Warnecke, Moonlit Ink
19 18 17 16 15   1 2 3 4 5

Library of Congress Cataloging-in-Publication Data
Apps, Jerold W., 1934–

  Whispers and shadows : a naturalist's memoir / Jerry Apps.
    pages cm

  ISBN 978-0-87020-709-9 (hardcover : alk. paper) — ISBN 978-0-87020-710-5 (e-book) 1. Apps, Jerold W., 1934– 2. Naturalists—Wisconsin—Biography. 3. Natural history—Wisconsin. I. Title.
  QH31.A64 A3 2015
  508.092—dc23
  [B]

                              2014039424

To Steve and Natasha

Contents

Introduction

Listen for the whispers and look in the shadows.

HERMAN APPS

My father loved nature. Well—he never used the word *love,* but his actions revealed how he felt louder than if he'd spoken the word. As a farmer, Pa worked outside in the heat of summer and the frigid days of winter. He felt no affection toward mosquitoes and wasps, and he didn't care much for dry weather or for blizzards, but he enjoyed nature in all of its manifestations.

Pa taught me about those things that are easily seen, heard, and smelled: the fragrant evidence of a skunk passing nearby, a crow calling in the far distance, a giant oak standing sentry on a hill. But he also impressed upon me the importance of listening for the whispers and looking in the shadows, of seeking out those things not easily witnessed: the tiniest wildflower, the subtle sound of snowflakes alighting on pine needles, the distant growl of thunder, a spider web hanging underneath a tuft of prairie grass. He taught me to observe those things that are often overlooked. He showed me that in the shadows and whispers reside bits of information that allow one to know something more deeply and profoundly.

From the time of my very earliest memories, I was connected to nature. I was born during the middle of the Great Depression on a small farm in central Wisconsin. Our nearest neighbors were the Millers, a half mile to the south, and the Davises, more than a half mile to the north; like us, they were farmers. Crowding up to the north side of our farmhouse was a twenty-acre woodlot made up mostly of black oaks and white oaks and home to an abundance of wood violets, wild geraniums, shrubs, squirrels, rabbits, and ruffed grouse. Here and there where the sunlight managed to filter through were patches of blackberries that tore at your skin when you waded in to pick the lush, fat purple berries.

A dirt road trailed past our farm. Oaks and elms and aspen lined both sides of the road from where it connected with "the north road" (country roads had no fancy names in those days) to County Road A to the south.

Our farm included 160 acres of land, 140 of which were available for cultivation. These fields had been farmed since the 1850s, and since this was where the last great glacier stopped, the land was studded with stones. As rocks of various sizes, colors, and shapes surfaced each spring, we toted them to the edges of the fields and piled them under the wire fences as the previous owners had done. Among the stones grew stunted oak trees, hazel brush, wild cherries, black raspberries, wild grapes, and an assortment of other plants and shrubs, creating a tangle of vegetation and offering shelter to a great variety of songbirds and wild animals that fed on the berries, found a home in hollow fence posts (bluebirds, in particular), and sought sanctuary among the stones.

The sixty acres of cultivated land nearest the farmstead was a hodgepodge of fields large and small, a barbwire fence surrounding each one. A lane twenty feet or so wide led from the barnyard to the farthest field, and along it our small herd of cattle, fifteen or twenty of them, walked to and from the barn twice a day for milking. Like the fields, the lane was lined with stones and trees and shrubs.

Like other farm kids of my generation, I grew up immersed in nature. I quickly discovered that the woodlot, just a few dozen steps from the kitchen door, was a place of great mystery and excitement. When I wasn't doing farm work, I spent hours in that old woods, sometimes sitting and listening, sometimes walking and looking for something that I hadn't seen before—a squirrel's nest, a hollow tree with a hole in it that had to be a raccoon's den, a new wildflower emerging from the forest floor.

As I walked the lane to fetch the cows from the pasture, I listened to the birds, watched for wild animals, kept track of when the berries were ripe—and helped myself to a few along the way. There were no roaring tractors to break the silence of a quiet, misty morning, no background traffic noise. For a farm kid alone with himself, it was a time for thinking and for enjoying the peaceful surroundings.

By the time I began first grade at age five (our country school had no kindergarten), I had a solid foundation in many facets of nature. I knew the difference between a white oak and a black oak; I knew the characteristics of white pine and aspen trees and how they grow. I could identify a black bass, a northern pike, a bluegill, and a yellow perch. I could tell the difference between the tracks of a rabbit, a squirrel, and a fox. I knew the call of a crow, the raucous jeer of a blue jay, and the lonesome, often eerie cry of an owl.

All these things I learned without realizing I was learning them. When I tagged along with my pa on his long Sunday walks or went fishing with him or simply stood next to him on the hill behind the barn at sunset, he pointed them out to me again and again. Pa had a vast understanding of nature's creatures and nature's ways, and he wanted me to learn them as well. But there was more to what he was doing than teaching me how to differentiate one creature from another, one track from another, one creature's call from another. Although he never said it in so many words, Pa wanted me to develop a love for nature that was as strong as his. He wanted me to learn the details of nature, but he also wanted me to *know* nature. Only years later did I begin to understand that there's a great difference between accumulating information about something—learning facts— and *knowing* something. Knowing is deeper. It takes a person to the place where beliefs and values reside. It is the foundation for appreciation. Knowing leads us to action, to caring for those things we know deeply and working to preserve them for future generations.

Now, many years later, I continue to listen for the whispers, look in the shadows, and strive to know nature. I know much, but I have much more to learn.

Today I own and operate a 120-acre farm called Roshara in Wisconsin's central sands region, just two miles from the farm where I grew up. On this land my family and I maintain a pine tree plantation, restore prairielands, preserve two small ponds and the surrounding wetlands, hunt for deer and wild turkeys, plant and care for a large garden, and hike and snowshoe its miles of trails. I've owned most of this property since 1966 (I added to it in 2011), and over these nearly five decades I have studied it, cared for it, and introduced my children and grandchildren to its history, its trees and flowers, and its wild creatures. I continue to be amazed by its many dimensions and the ways it has influenced me. My hope is that Roshara will have the same effect on my grandchildren; I know it has on my children.

For me, nature is everything that is not the product of human endeavor. It includes the land, water, and air, all the wild creatures, plants from the tallest oak trees to the tiniest wildflowers, weather, climate, drought, storms, wind, rain. On these pages I share some of my experiences with nature, from my childhood to today. I do so in the hope that these stories might spark an interest in others to become involved with nature. I believe that the more people know about something, the more likely they are to prize it, protect it, and encourage others to do so as well. The more deeply we come to know our natural surroundings, the more willing we are to stand up and be heard when a wetland is threatened by development, an endangered species' habitat faces destruction, or mature trees are in danger of being cut down because they are "in the way" of a new road.

Long ago I discovered that learning by doing is one of the best ways to learn. In the effort to get better acquainted with nature, "doing" can take many forms, from taking a walk in the woods to developing a personal nature philosophy. It can be as simple as bird-watching, learning to identify trees or wildflowers, taking a grandchild fishing or teaching her how to grow a vegetable garden, or sitting on a hillside on a warm summer evening and watching the sun set. Action helps us move beyond the belief that we live apart from nature—or, even more foolishly, that we can control nature. The truth is we cannot live apart from nature; indeed, we are *part of* nature. Our lives are intricately related to the lives of other living creatures. We depend on the land, water, and air for our very existence. As for any attempts on our part to control nature, we need only think of the tornados and hurricanes, droughts and floods, and blizzards that have brought communities to their knees— nature's reminders that it is not about to be controlled.

I also believe that nature is not an abstract idea to be read or debated or shouted about in headlines when it appears to be an obstacle to a new building, road, mine, or other human endeavor. To me, nature is personal, concrete, and specific. It has many dimensions and offers myriad opportunities for learning. But it also includes elements of the unknown and the unknowable. It is that mystery, that profound quality, that makes its study so endlessly fascinating.

The Home Place

Be it ever so humble, there's no place like home.

JOHN HOWARD PAYNE

As it does for most everyone, the place where I grew up established in large measure who I am today. During those years I spent growing up on the farm, walking, fishing, and exploring the countryside nearly every day, learning about nature came as naturally as breathing. Indeed, I think of the home place as one of my earliest teachers.

But when I left for college in 1951, I was determined to leave the home place behind. I did not want my classmates and instructors at the University of Wisconsin to know that I had grown up without electricity or indoor plumbing in a drafty farmhouse heated by woodstoves. I did not want them to know that I had driven a team of horses, attended a one-room country school, milked cows by hand, and hunted for the squirrels and cottontail rabbits that were an important part of our diet. I was determined to become a cosmopolitan urban person.

Despite my efforts, during the first week of classes a classmate pointed out to me that I walked like I was "walking behind a plow." With that I vowed to "walk city." By the time I graduated from the university in 1955, I felt like the urban person I was trying to become.

My perspective changed when I went into the army at age twenty-one the following year. During my training I quickly realized that my farm background had provided me some valuable skills. Unlike many of my army buddies from urban places, I was comfortable with a rifle, having used one since I was ten years old. The outdoors was my friend; indeed, I much preferred being there than in a stuffy army barracks. I didn't mind getting up early in the morning. I was accustomed to primitive living conditions. And even with a leg harmed by polio, I was physically strong and I knew how to work—a lesson all farm kids learn early. I had learned from my father the importance of doing a job well, no matter what that job might be. It dawned on me how wrong I had been to deny my upbringing, to try to disregard the influence of the home place on who I was, what I believed, and what I valued.

Young people today, especially those growing up in urban settings, have few opportunities to experience nature directly as I did. Those of us who know the importance of experiencing nature must encourage young people to occasionally leave their cell phones behind and walk in the woods, go fishing, tend a vegetable garden, or simply sit quietly where they can observe the natural world. Giving children a solid foundation of direct experiences with nature is one way to ensure that they will grow up to appreciate, enjoy, and protect it for future generations.

Walking

In every walk with nature one receives far more than he seeks.

JOHN MUIR

One of my first memories is of loading my teddy bear into my little red wagon and following the wagon tracks made by the team and wagon when Pa traveled to the far corner of the farm, where he and a hired man were digging potatoes. No doubt I wanted to help Pa haul the potatoes back to the farmstead with my wagon, and of course I needed my Ted along for company. The potato patch was a half mile from our farmhouse, but what did I know about distance? I was only three years old.

When I was growing up, if we wanted to go someplace within a mile or two, we walked. We walked not for exercise but with a purpose and a destination in mind: to visit a sick neighbor, to see how the crops were growing, to consider whether the cow pasture was still large enough for our small herd of dairy cows, to confirm that a recent storm had toppled a tree across a wire fence.

During the warm seasons, Pa and I walked nearly every Sunday afternoon. Our 160-acre farm was laid out in a square, a half mile on each side, so when we walked the entire perimeter of the farm we covered two miles. But we didn't keep track. There were no pedometers, and we made no attempts to record—or even talk about—how far we had walked. Instead we'd report to Ma what we had seen or heard: a fox den in a fencerow, a bluebird nest in a hollow post, the distant call of a bobwhite quail.

Eventually my twin brothers were old enough to join Pa and me, and we ranged farther on our Sunday walks. In those days there were few NO TRESPASSING signs, and we often wandered far from the home farm, checking on the neighbors' crops or simply exploring something that Pa had decided would be interesting to see. We saw, we listened, we tasted, we smelled, and we touched things. Pa didn't just show us something; he insisted that we get acquainted with it, which meant using more than our eyes.

By the time I was five or six years old, I often wandered off alone to the far corners of our farm during my free time. I was privileged to have parents who supported my wanderings, and I was blessed to have a father who loved nature deeply. Of course, he never talked about it that way. It was his actions that gave him away.

Ma's Garden

To forget how to dig the earth and to tend the soil
is to forget ourselves.

MAHATMA GANDHI

My mother's vegetable garden was located not far from the back door of our farmhouse, in a sunny spot where our backyard ended and the woods to the north began. Ma was in charge of the garden from the time she ordered seeds in January until the last pumpkin was stored in the cellar in October. In spring, Pa plowed and disked the garden plot with the team; after that he appeared in the garden only when Ma requested his help with cultivating, hoeing, or harvesting.

My first memory of helping Ma in her garden is a morning spent planting seeds in the freshly turned soil. I was probably no older than three. I was carefully placing bean seeds—which were large enough that I could grasp them easily with my little fingers—just the right distance apart in the trench Ma had made with a hoe along the marked row. Ma was a taskmaster; I had to place the seeds properly or do it over. She never yelled at me, just firmly told me, "There's a right way and a wrong to plant bean seeds, and I want you to learn the right way."

I can still see the big smile on Ma's face as she worked under the warm May sun. She told me, "Beans should never be planted before Decoration Day" (as Memorial Day was called in those days). The same held true for cucumbers, pumpkins, squash, and late sweet corn. With the beans planted, Ma moved on to cucumbers, making holes in the soil and telling me to put four cucumber seeds in each hole—not three, not five, but four. Not only was I learning how to plant cucumber seeds, I was practicing the counting skills that Ma had been teaching me.

When my brothers were old enough to work in the garden, they too learned how to plant, care for, and harvest garden crops the right way and at just the right time. Without knowing it, we were also learning how important our garden was for our family's food supply, as it provided all of the vegetables we ate throughout the year.

As I grew older I spent less time working with my mother in the garden and more time working beside Pa in the barn and the fields. But I still helped with weeding and harvesting. Time spent working in the garden was my best opportunity to be with my mother, to talk with her and learn from her.

Ma always planted several long rows of green beans, and she was a stickler about picking them at just the right time. The pods had to be firmly formed but still completely green. If they showed even a hint of yellow, they were too mature. Depending on the weather, we picked them every three or four days starting in July and continuing well into August. She also had rules for how to pick them. "Be gentle with the bean plant," she admonished. She was right. Bean plants do not have strong root systems, and a heavy tug on a bean pod could lift the entire plant from the ground—something I never wanted to do in Ma's presence. We picked the beans into pails, taking enough for several meals of freshly prepared beans for the table and for canning. It was hard, backbreaking work, but I was happy to be working outside, where I could hear birds singing and feel a cool breeze on my sweaty brow.

When we finished picking for the day, Ma spread an old newspaper on the kitchen table and dumped out the beans. Then we began preparing them for our table or for the canning jars. We sat across from each other at the table with a huge pile of beans between us. First we snipped off both ends of the bean pod; then we cut the bean into inch-long pieces that we dropped into a pan we held in our laps. One bean at a time, *snip, snip, snip.* As hard as I tried, I could never do it as fast as Ma.

Cutting green beans was one of the most boring jobs I ever had, ranking right up there with hoeing endless rows of potatoes, piling hay into bunches, and splitting stove wood. The one upside of the project was having time to talk with Ma. She could cut beans and talk without missing a beat. As we worked, she asked me questions: "Are you looking forward to school starting again?" "What subjects do you like best?"

Her questions got me thinking about something other than the formidable task of cutting a huge pile of green beans into little pieces. "I like school," I told her. "My favorites are reading, science, math, spelling, and history."

She smiled at my answers. "I liked spelling, too," she said. "I always wanted to be a teacher."

I'd never heard her say that before. "You did?"

"Yes, I thought it would be fun to teach in a country school. But I never did, because I never had a chance to go to high school." A sad look came over her face then. She continued snipping beans. "What do you want to do when you finish school?" she asked.

"Maybe be a farmer, like Pa," I answered.

It was quiet in the kitchen, except for the sounds of bean pieces dropping into our pans.

"It's a good life, but a hard life," she said after a moment. "But you can spend time outdoors, appreciate the quiet, and be close to nature."

"I like that," I said.

As we talked, the pile of beans shrank—much more quickly than I had thought it would.

When I think back to those times when Ma and I worked together in her garden, I realize how much she taught me, from how to plant seeds, to the best times and methods for harvesting, to how to prepare vegetables for canning. More important, I learned about the respect she had for the land and how her careful attention to the land directly resulted in food for our table. She may never have gotten to be a classroom teacher, but she was doing more teaching than she ever realized.

Trees

Alone among living things, [a tree] retains
its character and dignity after death.

As a farm kid in central Wisconsin, I grew up surrounded by trees of all sorts. From the time I was as young as three or four, some of them held special meaning for me.

In a misshapen old apple tree in front of our farmhouse, Pa fashioned a swing from a piece of rope and an oak board he found in the shed where he stored extra lumber. I spent many summer days in my swing when Ma wasn't after me to gather eggs, fetch wood for the cookstove, or retrieve a jar of peaches or strawberry jam from the cellar.

Behind our house, a grand elm shaded the back porch and the entryway to the kitchen. At noon during the summer, while we waited for Ma to announce that dinner was ready (dinner was what we called the midday meal), we gathered in the shade of that big elm and rested. After dinner, stuffed and unable to eat another bite, we pushed away from the table, walked outside, and sprawled again in the shade of the elm to nap for a half hour or so before returning to whatever summer task demanded our attention. On summer evenings, when the milking and other chores were done, the five of us sat on the back porch, listening to the sounds of early evening: the call of the whip-poor-will, the robin's twilight song, and the quiet rustling of the old elm's leaves as the shadows slowly engulfed us.

It was under that big elm tree that the threshing crews gathered after eating a big thresher's dinner to rest, swap stories, and catch up on neighborhood news. We entertained city relatives under the old elm on hot Sunday afternoons when they drove over from Wisconsin Rapids to visit. Because our farmhouse stood on a hill, in addition to enjoying the shade we often felt a gentle, cooling breeze as well.

I had always been an admirer of trees, but when I was eleven I became a steward of trees. That year, members of our community organized a 4-H club, which I eagerly joined. One of the first projects I signed up for was forestry. I was given fifty pine seedlings, each just a couple inches tall, that I was to plant in a tree nursery I had to make myself. I selected a spot in back of the chicken house and planted the trees with a planting board that I constructed according to the 4-H project manual instructions. The board was six inches wide, and I cut notches in it one inch apart. Thus, I planted the trees in my pine nursery one inch apart in rows six inches apart.

I checked on my little trees every morning on my way to the barn to see how they were faring, and when dry weather set in I diligently carried water from the pump house to water them. They grew well. But one morning when I arrived at my tree nursery, about a third of the trees were uprooted, their fragile roots drying in the morning sun. I quickly replanted them, hoping to save as many as possible. I determined that Ma's chickens had decided the moist soil in my tree nursery was a good place to look for earthworms and had dug up my trees in their search for lunch. Pa helped me erect a wire fence around the tree nursery, which solved the problem.

After two years in the nursery, my trees were ready to be moved to a permanent location. I planted them in an open area on the north end of our woodlot, spacing them six feet apart and in rows eight feet apart. Today, more than sixty-five years later, those trees are more than fifty feet tall and still growing. Although my family doesn't own the land anymore, I often drive by and marvel at how well the trees have done since they arrived at the farm as tiny stems that scarcely stuck out of the ground when I planted them.

I still have trees that are special to me. The most prized is a maple growing in the yard in front of the cabin at Roshara, a gift from my three children on my sixtieth birthday. When the tree was a couple years old and around six feet tall, we almost lost it. That October a whitetail buck, eager to remove the velvet from its antlers, attacked the tree and scraped off a goodly portion of its bark. The tree survived, but with a considerable scar on its side. Now thirty or more feet tall, the maple provides wonderful shade in summer and a glorious display of fall color.

Not far from my prized birthday maple is a row of enormous black willow trees, planted in 1912 by John Coombes, then the owner of this land. A bit out of their element (black willows prefer lower land with more moisture), these willows nevertheless grew to serve as a windbreak for the farm buildings, slowing down the cold westerly and northwesterly winds that sweep across the landscape in winter. Today these old willows, misshapen and missing branches sacrificed to the strong winds, continue to protect my buildings. They also serve as a home to untold numbers of songbirds and squirrels. Under the trees, in underbrush that I have never cleared, cottontail rabbits make their home, along with the occasional ruffed grouse, woodchucks, thirteen-striped ground squirrels (also known as gophers), and other critters.

Planted as a windbreak during the Dust Bowl era, a stately row of white pines stands in the field south of the cabin. They remind me of those awful days in the 1930s when the sky was filled with brown dust on windy days. The sandy soil of this farm, plowed in those years by John Coombes and his son, Weston, with hopes of raising a crop of corn or oats, soared into the sky and drifted to the east.

Today those white pines are fifty and sixty feet tall, three to four feet in diameter. They've served their purpose as a windbreak, for along the western edge of the row of pines is a hump of soil, two or more feet high in places, that the winds blew off my fields to the west. Today I often sit under those old trees, listening to the quiet rustling of their needles, smelling the wonderful fragrance of evergreen, and simply thinking or not thinking. My most joyful time under the pines—in their eighties now and likely to live for at least another hundred years—is spent watching the sun set.

On the western edge of my prairie stands a lone black oak, probably planted by a squirrel and then forgotten. On hot summer evenings I relax under this tree, looking out over my prairie and its ever-changing array of native grasses and wildflowers. The tree isn't large, and it's not old either—maybe only forty, a youngster among black oaks, which can live two hundred years or more. But it provides excellent shade on hot days.

Of all the trees that grow at Roshara, I am most impressed by the bur (or burr) oaks. These tough trees withstand fire, storms, dry weather, wet weather; they come through it all and continue growing year after year, up to eighty feet tall or even taller, some living for two or three hundred years. The bur oak's hardiness can be attributed to its tremendous root system, which can grow to a depth of twenty feet and a lateral spread of forty feet. In other words, what you see of the tree aboveground is only about half of it. They are not especially attractive, with thick, corky bark and scraggly limbs going this way and that, but bur oaks have their own unique beauty. Besides, bur oaks are native to this farm. No one hauled them in from somewhere else. They have thrived in much of central and southwestern Wisconsin as long as any living things have been here.

Jack pines are native to this area as well, and just as tough. I've never seen a deer chew on a jack pine or seen any other critter giving them grief. They grow where grass won't and where no other trees would stand a chance. The coldest of winters and the hottest of summers seem not to faze them. The jack pine is a survivor in challenging habitats. I like that in a tree.

Too often these days trees are considered a nuisance—seen as standing in the way of development, or messy because they drop leaves and seeds, or feared because a storm might drop one onto a home or other structure. Others see trees only in economic terms, as sources of lumber for construction, pulp for the paper industry, Christmas trees to decorate our homes, or firewood to feed our stoves and fireplaces. Of course, trees do have economic value, but their worth extends far beyond that, as their beauty and spiritual contributions make our lives richer and more fulfilled.

While I enjoy individual trees and species, I am truly amazed by a woodlot, where trees and shrubs, wildflowers and ferns, birds and animals live together in a natural community, depending on each other but also competing for sunlight, nutrients, and moisture. A woodlot can be seen as a metaphor for all of nature, a complex tangle of life existing together and influenced by weather, geography, and geology. The individual elements of a woodlot can be identified, labeled, and studied in depth. But the woodlot is much more than the sum of its parts.

When I was a boy, the twenty-acre woodlot that lay just outside our back door was an endless source of fascination for me. It took on even more significance in my life after I contracted polio at age twelve. Suddenly I was a farm kid who could no longer play ball, run and jump and swim, walk for miles without tiring, or take care of my farm work.

With a paralyzed right leg, I couldn't even stand up without holding on to something. I felt I was worthless, and I was sure everyone around me thought the same. When I had regained enough strength in my bad leg to hobble along, I went to our woodlot, where I would simply sit on a stump for an hour or longer. Trees don't care if you can't walk or play ball. They are forgiving, there to comfort and provide solace. Whenever I felt especially down—which was often, during my recovery—I would escape to the woods. I have never forgotten how much that woodlot did for me.

Today my sixty-acre woodlot at Roshara contains a vast collection of bur oak, black oak, white oak, quaking aspen, white pine, red pine, largetooth aspen, birch, black cherry, and spruce. Just as I did when I was a boy, I wander into the woodlot and just sit and listen. I like to believe that the trees are talking to me. The white pine has a soft, quiet message when a breeze caresses its needles; the quaking aspen, its small leaves all aflutter in a breeze, makes a more nervous sound. In the winter, when the bare branches lift toward an often gray sky, I listen to the northwest wind making its moaning, sorrowful sound as it moves through the dormant tree limbs and rattles the dead oak leaves that will not fall until spring.

I go to my woodlot to gather my thoughts and to realize how insignificant I am among these towering oaks, for my woodlot has always been a woodlot, since the last glacier formed this land more than ten thousand years ago.

The woodlot is so much more than an economic asset. It is where I go when the world seems to tumble down around me, when the pressures of my work seem overwhelming, and when things are going well and I want to celebrate my good fortune. Trees are good listeners. They don't argue. They don't talk back. And they are always there.

Wildflowers and Other Plants

Something fascinating happens in the prairie restoration at my farm: almost every summer, a wildflower I've never seen before mysteriously appears. My sense of wonder kicks in. Were the seeds present in the soil all along, just waiting for the proper conditions to germinate? Did a bird drop a seed in this spot? Or was the flower always there and I just wasn't observant enough to see it? I dig out my guidebooks and search for the newfound flower. I learn its history, its growing conditions and range, its unique features. When my grandkids are with me, as they often are, finding a flower in the wild and then learning about it in a guidebook is a wonderful, eye-opening experience. Such is the joy of becoming acquainted with all that nature has to offer—and often being totally surprised at what is discovered.

Wood violets

The first wildflower whose name I learned was the wood violet. One Saturday in May when I was just three or four years old, my father walked with me to a patch of wood violets on the far end of our woodlot. The next day was Mother's Day, and Pa said we should surprise my mother with a bouquet. There, in the partial shade of old black and white oaks, we picked a small bunch of the beautiful lavender and purple flowers.

When I presented them to Ma, she gave me a big hug and put the violets in a jelly jar she filled with water. She placed the bouquet in the center of our kitchen table. During those waning years of the Great Depression, there was no money for presents—but Ma didn't seem to mind that I had not given her a store-bought gift.

The wood violet has been one of my favorite wildflowers ever since. They appear on my farm each spring to remind me of my childhood.

Wild roses

My farm is located in Rose Township, and the nearest village is Wild Rose. Both are said by some to have been named for Rose, New York, where many of the settlers to this area originally lived. But others believe these places were named after the wild roses that grow here.

Last summer I was driving my ATV along the prairie trail when I spotted a splash of pink. I stopped and discovered a sizeable patch of wild roses growing among the tangle of prairie grass on a droughty hillside. I hadn't seen wild roses in that spot before; the last ones I had seen had grown alongside the trail to the pond but had been snuffed out by the competitive buckthorn that grows everywhere these days.

The wild rose has five light pink petals and a soft but distinctive aroma. No other rose, in my judgment, comes close to the wonderful smell of the wild rose, and I have grown cultivated roses for many years. The person who coined the phrase "Stop and smell the roses" surely had the wild rose in mind.

Goldenrods

When goldenrods were in full flower on the home farm, we all admired their color and welcomed their reminder that fall was around the corner. But Pa appreciated goldenrods for another reason. After we'd had several hard frosts, we would visit the goldenrod patches, by that time dead and brown, and look for goldenrod galls, growths on the plants' stems about the size of a golf ball, sometimes smaller. Nestled within each gall was a quarter-inch-long white grub: the larvae of the goldenrod fly, which had deposited its eggs in the stem of the plant back in late summer. The larvae fed on the inside of the stem, causing the stem to enlarge and thus creating the gall. Pa wanted the grubs for ice fishing, as they were excellent bait for bluegills, perch, and other pan fish.

There are more than one hundred species of goldenrod. Whenever I try to identify which kinds grow at Roshara, I get a bit overwhelmed by the many varieties. By early September in most years, my prairie is a sea of goldenrod yellow, lasting until the first frost. It's quite a sight to see.

Black-eyed Susans

Black-eyed Susans have been special at Roshara since our daughter, Susie, called them black-eyed Susies when she was a little girl. These striking plants grow two to three feet tall and have daisylike flowers, yellow with brown centers. Black-eyed Susans take care of themselves, and they seem to like my sandy, gravelly prairie soil—I have not planted one black-eyed Susan seed since we began our prairie restoration, yet they grow in abundance here and come back year after year.

Wild geraniums

Wild geraniums should not be confused with cultivated geraniums; in fact, they're nothing alike. At Roshara, wild geraniums grow along the trail near the pond, no more than eighteen inches tall and with dainty lavender flowers that appear in spring. They grow in the shadows and can be easily overlooked. But I look for them every spring, hopeful that a deer hasn't chewed them off and that they have not succumbed to dry weather, too much shade, or a host of other factors that challenge wildflowers. So far, so good.

Lupines

One early June day I found a small patch of long-stemmed plants with blue flowers growing on a sandy side hill on the south side of the farm. It was unfamiliar to me—I'd never seen it as a kid on the home farm—and I immediately dug out my flower identification book. I determined that I am lucky enough to have lupines at Roshara. At one time considered a robber of soil nutrients, the lupine was named after lupus, the voracious wolf. In actuality lupines are beneficial legumes that fix nitrogen in the soil.

My son Steve and I cleared away some scotch pine and brushy shrubs growing just to the southeast of the lupine patch, and within five years the patch had grown to a few acres. The flowers seem to flourish on our droughty, sandy soils. By late May or early June, our lupine patch is a sea of blue flowers nodding in the spring breeze. When the lupine seed pods are ripe, by early July, they pop open and the prevailing southwest winds scatter the seeds for a considerable distance, sometimes fifty yards or more.

The lupine plays an important role in the reproduction of the Karner blue butterfly, a federally designated endangered species. The Karner's entire life cycle is dependent on the lupine. The butterflies lay their eggs on the leaves of stems; when the eggs hatch, the larvae eat lupine leaves—and only lupine leaves—until they form their chrysalises. As our lupine patch has grown, so has our Karner blue population. We have seen as many as fifty Karners fluttering about at a time.

Lilacs

Pa didn't like lilacs—he said he didn't like how they smelled—so we had none on our home farm. But a long row of lilacs grew along the southern stretch of the fence surrounding our country school. The bushes were tall and thick, and during the last weeks of school in May they were covered with beautiful, sweet-smelling flowers. Our teacher always had a fresh bouquet on her desk, the flowers' fragrance turning the schoolroom's lingering smoky smell of winter into the sweet smell of spring.

Since then I've always liked lilacs, and when we bought Roshara in 1966 I was pleased to find a long row of them growing near the remnants of the farm buildings. The Coombes family must have liked lilacs too, for they planted three kinds: dark purple, lavender, and a very tall white variety. My best guess is that they planted them in 1912, around the time they constructed the buildings. Now, more than a hundred years later, we keep a big bouquet of lilacs on the cabin table in May, their sweet perfume crowding out the smell of wood smoke after the long winter.

Wild grapevines

The wild grapevines at Roshara crawl over the lilac bushes by the cabin. They climb nearly to the top of the oak trees that line the trail to the pond. They curl up the red cedar by the machine shed. And they have succeeded in climbing to the peak of the pump house, nearly covering the east wall of the building. I have no idea how old these grapevines are, but near the pond I have found vines that are as big around as my wrist and more than forty feet long. Sometimes we harvest the wild grapes, which are tiny but in wet years are abundant. Too often, though, the birds harvest them before we have an opportunity.

My grapevines are aggressive and exploratory. One mischievous vine snuck through a crack in a pump house window. Once inside, the curious vine discovered that no sunlight reaches the depths of the dark and dreary pump house, now used mainly as a woodshed. So the vine crawled along the south interior wall, found a crack above the door, and exited to the outside where it was once more treated to the afternoon sun. It appears happy as can be and seems rather proud that it has crawled in and back out of the pump house. I must say, I am impressed.

Big bluestem grass

As a kid I was always fascinated by pioneer stories, tales of families traveling west in covered wagons pulled by oxen. When they arrived in the Midwest in the early 1800s, they encountered the tallgrass prairies, big bluestem grass growing as high as their oxen or higher, waves of grass as far as the eye could see. According to some travelers' accounts, they felt they were seeing a great prairie ocean, the wind playing over the grass as it might over a great body of water.

Not long after acquiring Roshara, I was hiking on a steep side hill at the back of the property when I came upon a strange and beautiful blue-green grass that was taller than me. We had many grasses on the home farm—quackgrass, timothy, blue grass, June grass, fox tail, reed canary grass, and others—but nothing like this. I would have noticed a grass that grows as tall as six or seven feet.

With a bit of research I identified the puzzling plant as native big bluestem grass. In fact, big bluestem, a prominent feature in the tall grass prairies of Illinois, Iowa, southern Minnesota, and the western states, had once grown over much of the land that is now my farm—pretty much anyplace that wasn't covered with trees. Native Americans used the root of the grass as a diuretic and to lessen stomach pains; they used an extract from the leaf blades to combat fever and as an analgesic; and they used the plant itself to tie together support poles for dwellings and to cover fruit while it was drying.

I wondered how a grass that can grow to seven feet tall could survive on this sandy, droughty side hill where I had found it. The answer: big bluestem is capable of sending roots down as far as ten feet in search of moisture. This is a plant that does well on heavy soils with lots of moisture; it also does reasonably well on poor soils with limited rainfall. And because this hill is so steep, it's likely the soil had never been plowed.

I wanted to know more about the big bluestem on my farm and how this onetime prairie had become a wheat field. I learned that in 1867, Tom Stewart, a Civil War veteran and native of New York state, acquired this land thanks to the Homestead Act of 1862. That law made federal lands available to settlers for the cost of a modest filing fee and with the requirement that they spend at least five years on the land "proving up"—building a cabin, living on the land, and actively farming it.

After Tom Stewart removed the scrub oak trees and hazel brush, he was ready to break the land, to turn under the acres of big bluestem that had grown on this sandy soil for hundreds, even thousands of years. Stewart hired the team of Ike Woodward and William Henry Jenks, who made their way from farm to farm with their teams of oxen and a breaking plow to open this new land for cultivation. Each man owned two yoke of oxen—eight animals total. The breaking plow, a massive machine with a white oak beam two feet thick and eighteen feet long and a five-foot-long moldboard of steel, turned the soil and cut a furrow twenty inches wide and eight or nine inches deep through the big bluestem's tangle of thick, tough roots. The plowmen managed to break about fifty acres of Stewart's hilly and stony land, but they left untouched the side hill too steep for plowing.

Now these many years later, every time I hike past the big bluestem remnant, I think of Tom Stewart and wonder what he must have thought when he first looked over this vast expanse of big bluestem grass studded with the occasional struggling oak. I think too of the Menominee Indians who passed by here on their trips across what is now Adams County to the trading post on the Fox River now called Berlin. Did they use the grass as other tribes had historically done? The big bluestem grass on my farm is a direct tie to an earlier time, a reminder of what the land was like before the pioneers arrived.

Animals

Like wind and sunsets, wild things were taken for granted
until progress began to do away with them.

ALDO LEOPOLD

We encounter a great variety of animals at Roshara: coyotes, little brown bats, badgers, skunks, raccoons, foxes,
bears, thirteen-striped ground squirrels (we call them gophers), red squirrels, chipmunks, woodchucks, wild mink,
otters, muskrats, field mice, and more. I'm told a wolf pack
wanders near here, but I haven't seen evidence of wolves
yet. We consider all of them our neighbors, even friends,
but as with our human neighbors, we sometimes have dis-
agreements. Ruth, my wife, is never happy when a field
mouse decides it wants to spend the winter in our cabin,
and I have had to put up a fence to keep the deer and raccoons out of my garden. I often think of the old saying
"Good fences make for good neighbors." The sentiment cer-
tainly applies to the deer and raccoons.

Cottontail rabbits

On our home farm, cottontail rabbits lived in the fencerows
and along the edges of our woodlot. They didn't bother us,

even when they ate the occasional corn plant or stole some lettuce or bean plants from my mother's vegetable garden; a missing plant here and there from Ma's large garden or the twenty-acre cornfield was no cause for concern.

Still, it was completely natural for us as farmers to both like and respect an animal and yet feel no qualms about having it for dinner. After all, we also cared for and had great respect for our chickens, hogs, and cattle; these too found their way to our table.

On a Sunday afternoon in the fall of the year, Pa and I would grab our .22 rifles and search out a rabbit or two for supper. Finding them was easiest, of course, when there was snow on the ground and we could follow their tracks. Pa insisted we shoot only if we could make a clean kill, which meant shooting the animal in the head. This was humane for the rabbit and also kept the bullet from harming any of the edible parts. I quickly learned never to shoot at a rabbit that is running—the chances of a clean kill are too slim.

I no longer hunt cottontails, although a goodly number of them live in my stone pile just west of the cabin. I enjoy watching them munching on my native grass lawn, though I'm not thrilled when a bunny helps itself to the green beans, lettuce, or other vegetables in my garden. But like my mother, I overplant many of my vegetables for that very reason.

One year the rabbits went too far and just about destroyed my bean patch. Drastic action was required. I bought a product called Liquid Fence, a concoction of rotten eggs, red peppers, and other nasties. I sprayed the awful-smelling stuff on my remaining bean plants, and they survived. It took several rainstorms before the plants quit smelling like rotten eggs, however.

Gray and fox squirrels

Both gray squirrels and fox squirrels lived in the oak woods north of the farmhouse where I grew up. It was easy to spot their large, twiggy, rather messy-looking nests up high in an oak tree, and we often heard them "barking" on cool fall afternoons. But spotting one, especially up close, was never easy. We hunted them for their meat, but the strategy for hunting squirrels was considerably different from that for rabbits. It required patience and the ability to remain quiet for a half hour or longer.

Pa and I hunted squirrels with our farm dog, Fanny, who was an excellent squirrel hunter. She too managed to show great patience as she sat with us on a cool, late fall Sunday afternoon. By the time Pa and I glimpsed a squirrel moving through the tops of the oaks, Fanny had already seen it. She would set out running toward the tree where she had spotted the squirrel and let out a couple of sharp barks. We would come on the run, our .22s at the ready. We had worked out an excellent system with Fanny (perhaps it was a system she worked out with us): when she barked up at that squirrel, the squirrel would move around to the other side of the tree away from Fanny. Of course, that's where we were standing ready with our rifles. Just as with rabbits, either we had a clean shot at the squirrel's head or we didn't shoot.

We took our quarry back home to Ma, who had some interesting recipes for preparing both fried squirrel and fried rabbit. She mixed up a breadcrumb coating, rubbed it on the meat, sprinkled it with salt and pepper, and then fried it with an ample amount of onion, a method that took away much of the gamey flavor of the meat. We enjoyed squirrel and rabbit meat throughout the fall, usually several times a week.

I don't hunt squirrels today, but I like watching them. If I sit quietly in my woodlot for a half hour or so, one or more squirrels usually appear, hopping along in the downed oak leaves or displaying their acrobatic prowess by jumping from branch to branch more than forty feet from the ground.

Whitetail deer

When I was a little tyke, there were no deer near our home farm. The closest deer population was in Adams County, some twenty miles away. There were many more in the northern counties of the state, and during those years avid hunters from our area rode a train north and spent the week in a ramshackle cabin in the Northwoods. They usually brought back big bucks with trophy racks and, according to Pa, "meat so tough you couldn't stick a fork into it or cut the gravy with a sharp knife."

Pa could not leave behind the twice-a-day every day milking required of dairy farmers, so he never went on these Northwoods treks. But he and Bill Miller, our nearest neighbor to the south, took hunting day trips to Adams County, and in most years venison supplemented our supply of squirrels and rabbits and home-raised pork.

When I was twelve, I joined Pa on his hunting trips. In those days there were hundreds of acres of abandoned farmland with open fields and jack pine woods everywhere, and the deer were few and far between. But the glaciated land of northern Adams County, so flat compared to the hills and valleys around our home farm, was so different and interesting to me that I spent more time looking around than paying attention to hunting deer, anyway. Pa liked hunting in Adams County for reasons that went far beyond the odds of bagging a deer. He was born in the Adams County township of Rome, and we hunted in an area he knew well from his childhood. On one of our trips he showed me the site of the log one-room school, now no longer standing, where he had gotten his early education.

At Roshara the whitetail deer often come right up to the cabin, nibbling the grass—and sometimes nibbling things they shouldn't, such as Ruth's flowers. But last June I saw something I had never seen before. I was walking a trail in the woodlot north of the cabin with my daughter, Susan, her husband, Paul, and my grandson Josh. We were enjoying the coolness of the deep woods and the fresh spring air when Susie spotted a big doe in the shadows on the trail ahead. We stopped, fell silent, and watched. Soon a fawn emerged from the underbrush, just a tiny thing no more than a couple feet tall. The fawn began nursing, its little white tail waving back and forth. All the while, the doe kept a wary eye turned toward us. After a few minutes the doe apparently decided she didn't like the look—or smell—of us, and she disappeared into the thick underbrush. Her fawn stood there alone for a moment and then abruptly turned and bounded after its mother. In all my years of watching deer, that was the first time I had seen a fawn nursing in the wild. We were captivated by the sight and knew it was something to be forever remembered.

Beavers

On my first deer-hunting trip, on a dark and dreary late November day, Pa assigned me to a spot on the Roch-A-Cri River, a good-sized stream that flows through the area.

"If you keep the river to your right, you won't get lost," Pa said. He wasn't the only one concerned about my getting lost; roads were few and far between in that part of Adams County in those days, and every field and jack pine woodlot looked the same to me. I wasn't sure how I would find my way back to Pa.

I've always been enthralled by rivers and ponds, perhaps because the home farm had neither. So I propped Pa's double-barrel 12-gauge against a jack pine and sat on the riverbank to watch the river. Before long I saw something swimming—something big, carrying a stick in its mouth. I wondered what a dog would be doing out there in the middle of nowhere, swimming in the river. As it came closer, I saw its big, flat tail. It was a beaver, of course, a mature one. I watched the animal swim toward a huge pile of sticks—a beaver dam that several beavers were building across the river using aspen trees, both trunks and limbs that they had cut. I was amazed at the beavers' ability to cut down trees, some more than six inches in diameter, using their teeth. I was also impressed with how hard they worked and how smart they were in putting together the dam.

Finally one of the beavers spotted me. It slapped its tail on the water, making a sound like a rifle shot. Immediately everything went quiet on the river. All the beavers had disappeared.

I must have watched the beavers working on their building project for most of an hour—although when I told Pa about what I had seen and heard, I made it sound like I had spent only a few minutes. And I didn't tell Pa this, but watching beavers was a whole lot more interesting than looking for an elusive deer.

Every few years, beavers show up at one of the ponds at Roshara. They cut down a few aspen trees, and one year they nearly completed a dam across one end of the pond we call Pond I. No water flows in or out of this small body of water, however, and eventually they abandoned the project, leaving behind their intricate work and no doubt going in search of a stream they could dam. I've seen ten-inch-diameter trees cut by beavers—no small task. I am impressed by their industriousness, if not their wisdom in selecting Pond I to dam.

Snapping turtles

Biologists say snapping turtles lived during the time of the dinosaurs. When you see one, you are seeing a bit of ancient history. The first time I met one up close—too close—

was when I was out cane-pole fishing with my pa and brothers in a wooden rowboat in Norwegian Lake. We had baited our hooks with earthworms and were hoping to snare a bluegill, a sunfish, or maybe a perch. But the fish weren't biting, and our big red-and-white bobbers stood motionless. We sat there for a half hour or so, Pa reminding us that the most important quality in a fisherman is patience. Pa also considered silence a great virtue, especially when fishing, hiking, hunting, or doing just about anything in nature, and he reminded me of that when I suggested we row to a different spot. Just as I was about to open my mouth to differ with Pa's judgment, it happened: Darrel's bobber dipped below the surface and never came up. Generally when a bluegill bites, it nibbles; the bobber goes under, bounces to the surface, and goes under again. But this time the bobber stayed under. Darrel lifted his long cane pole to tighten the line and began pulling in the fish. The pole bent. Pa looked both interested and concerned.

"Move the pole around so I can grab the line," he said. I could tell from the look on his face that he thought Darrel's pole was about to break, as cane poles are prone to do when too much is asked of them. Now Pa was pulling on the thick green fishing line, hand over hand. The line stayed tight, jerking occasionally. Pa kept pulling. My brothers and I peered into the depths of the lake to see what kind of monster fish was about to surface. After what seemed like a long, long time—but probably was less than a minute—we saw what Darrel had hooked. Coming up from the depths was the most gruesome-looking creature I had ever seen, shaped like a big washtub, dark gray, its back covered with moss. It had a long, thick neck, four legs with long claws, and a scaly tail.

"What is it?" I shouted as the menacing-looking creature came closer to the boat.

"Snapper," Pa said calmly. "Snapping turtle. A mean bugger."

"What do I do?" Darrel asked. He sounded like he wasn't sure he wanted to share the boat with this mossy-backed creature from the depths.

"I'll cut the line," Pa said, and he did. The big snapper took one last look at us with its beady eyes and settled once more out of sight.

Many years later I was hiking on one of the hillsides above one of our ponds when I came upon a snapping turtle. The big female was laying eggs in a hole she had scratched into the sandy soil. Doing a little research afterwards, I learned that a snapping turtle lays as many as twenty-five to fifty eggs, which take from nine to eighteen weeks to incubate, depending on the soil temperature. I also learned that turtle eggs are a delicacy for foxes, coyotes, and skunks. This was confirmed for me when I returned to the site and discovered several holes that once had held snapping turtle eggs; all that remained were a few leathery eggshells and the promise of a diminished snapping turtle population.

Snapping turtles are not friendly, cuddly creatures; they are powerful predators that spend their forty-year life span feasting on plants and animals that are convenient targets for their sharp jaws and their appetites, including frogs, fish, and newly hatched ducks and geese. But as fierce as they are, snapping turtles are not safe from attack. One spring a couple years ago, while exploring on the far side of our pond, I found a snapping turtle on its back. Weighing ten or fifteen pounds, with yellowish legs and sharp, curving claws, the snapper had bite marks on its thick neck and on its shell. It was nearly dead. Had it become a snack for a coyote? A day later, we found the dead snapper. Its shell became a specimen for Paul, my teacher son-in-law, to share with his science class.

Moose

Wisconsin boasts a few moose in the north, near the border with Upper Michigan. But sightings of them are rare here. I never saw one in the wild until I began canoeing in northern Minnesota's Boundary Waters Canoe Area Wilderness. And even then I had never seen one up close—until the time Steve and I got a little *too* close.

We had spent a week camping in the Boundary Waters, enjoying good weather and reasonably good fishing. On this trip we had seen bald eagles, loons, even a few beavers, but nary a moose. On our last day we got up early, took down our tents, and packed our equipment into our Duluth packs in the dark. It was a long drive back to Madison, and we had a couple hours of paddling before we would arrive at our parked car.

As is often the case in late summer, the warm water collided with the cool predawn air to create fog over the lake. We paddled along for a half hour without incident, Steve in the back steering and me in the front looking out for rocks. The sun struggled to break through the fog and mist slowly lifting from the glassy water. With more sunlight it became easier to spot rocks ahead of us. As I called out "Rock to the left" or "Rock to the right," Steve made the appropriate corrections in our direction of travel.

Then I saw an enormous one. "Rock dead on," I said to Steve. He swerved to go around it.

"Rock is getting bigger," I said, surprised.

"Can't be," answered Steve.

But the rock was growing larger. And then it wasn't a rock at all, but an enormous bull moose that had been feeding on plants on the lake bottom. Slowly the animal emerged, not a hundred feet from us.

"What should I do?" asked Steve.

"Nothing. Let's just quit paddling and hope for the best," I replied.

So we sat, our heavily loaded canoe riding low in the water, our paddles motionless. The moose came ever closer. It had the most magnificent antlers I've ever seen—a rack that, with a flick of the animal's head, would upset our canoe and send us swimming to escape the beast.

The big bull ignored us. He made his way to shore, climbed out of the water, shook himself like a big dog might, and disappeared into the underbrush. Steve and I looked at each other, shook our heads in disbelief, and commenced paddling. We had seen our moose for this trip. We were both amazed that we'd been so close to the magnificent creature that we could see the water weeds hanging from its rack.

Birds

A forest bird never wants a cage.

HENRIK IBSEN

We do not lack for birds at our farm in central Wisconsin. Some stay all year, braving the cold winters. Others spend just their summers with us. As the years have passed, we've noticed that some of our favorites are fewer in number, and some, such as the northern bobwhite and the meadowlark that I remember so well from my childhood, have disappeared entirely, likely due to the loss of their natural habitat. A few species have noticeably increased in numbers: Canada geese, sandhill cranes, and cardinals.

Since the bear population in central Wisconsin has grown, we use our birdfeeder only during the winter months when the bears are in hibernation (bears love birdseed). That means we no longer get to see the summer birds at our feeder, but we continue to enjoy them in the wild.

Canada geese

I remember standing with Pa out back of the barn on a cool November afternoon, watching the Canada geese pass high overhead and hearing Pa say, "Weather's about to change. Geese know it first."

To this day I'm impressed by migrating geese. Every time I see a high-flying flock, I relax, knowing that at least one thing is still right with the world. The seasons are changing, and the geese know it first.

In recent years a pair of Canada geese has nested on one of my ponds. I watch them often, amazed by how they can land in the pond with almost no noise, their wings set and their webbed feet braced in front of them just before they settle on the water.

I like to watch the goslings, all fluffy and fragile, paddling behind their mother as they search for breakfast. The gander, a bit larger than his lifelong mate, watches for danger.

A couple of years ago, after a chilly and windy fall night, I hiked to the pond shortly after daybreak. As I drew closer I heard the chatter of many geese. Goose talk while the flock is resting and feeding sounds rather like a flock of chickens, a clucking that's very different from the distinctive honks we usually associate with Canada geese.

I walked slowly, trying to make not a sound as I approached through the mist rising from the water, which was still warmer than the early morning air. When I could finally see through the thickets of brush and tall grass growing around the pond, I spotted the flock. The geese must have been flying south when the strong winds sent them looking for a safe place to spend the night, find something to eat, and wait for the wind to die down.

I spotted the guard goose, a large gander that stood on

the bank of the pond, looking around, on alert, ready to announce any dangers. Either he hadn't spotted me (unlikely), or he had quickly seen that I did not have a gun and posed no danger, as he did not sound the alarm.

Canada geese are intelligent. One of their most remarkable traits is their ability to migrate long distances, often in rain and wind, and return to the same place where they lived the year before. I believe the same pair of Canada geese has nested in almost the exact same spot at my pond for several years.

I also marvel at their social structure, in which the flock designates (how?) one bird to be in charge of security—is it the head goose, or is this merely a task assigned by some superior goose in the chain of command? I have many unanswered questions about these beautiful birds.

Bald eagles

It was a wintery day in mid-February, and the road near my farm was slippery and snow covered. I drove along slowly, keeping an eye out for traffic and planning what I would do if I met another driver. Up ahead in a bare patch in the road I spotted something big and white—a white jacket someone had lost?

When I was within a few feet of it, it moved, and then it leaped into the air on giant wings. I'm sure my mouth dropped open, for I had just crossed paths with a bald eagle feasting on a roadkill deer. Its white tail was spread wide, and its white head turned my way with a "get along with you so I can get back to my lunch" look. In the last two or three years, I have occasionally spotted an eagle sitting in a tree alongside the road near my pond and once, a year ago, soaring over Pond I, white tail and head clearly visible. So far I've not found an eagle's nest at Roshara.

I recall the dreadful time in the late 1950s and 1960s when the population of bald eagles and other raptors was in rapid decline. Then Rachel Carson's memorable book *Silent Spring*, published in 1962, revealed that the culprit was the pesticide dichlorodiphenyltrichloroethane, or DDT. In the 1960s, Wisconsin conservationists and concerned citizens led the nation in identifying the drastic effects of DDT on bald eagles and other birds. Activists led protests, gathered signatures on petitions, and helped the nation realize that this popular pesticide was devastating an entire category of wildlife. A substantial group of deniers refused to accept the science proving what DDT was doing to the wild bird population, but science eventually won out, and nearly all use of DDT was banned. The bald eagle population has been on the increase ever since.

Robins

Members of the thrush family, robins are one of the earliest birds to arrive in the spring and among the last to leave in the fall. Their sprightly call on a warm March day, always optimistic and uplifting, is a signal that although there still may be patches of snow on the ground, spring is almost here. The robins know it, and they are not shy about telling everyone.

I like to watch these birds searching for earthworms in

the mostly untended lawn at my farm. Their hearing must be acute, for they cock their heads to the side just before drilling into my sandy lawn and retrieving a fat earthworm for lunch. I know when I see them gathering in large numbers in the fall that winter isn't far off.

House wrens

House wrens are small and brown and feisty, with a rather long bill and a longish tail that is usually cocked high. And oh, how they can sing. As the sun is coming up on a spring morning and the mist is rising, the first sound I hear filtering through my cabin bedroom window is the song of the wren. Several pairs live around the cabin, in wren houses we have constructed and in other spots as well. They don't seem to be choosy about where they build their nests. I have even found wren nests built on top of bluebird nests in my bluebird houses after the bluebirds have moved on. Why seek out a new nesting place when an established one is available?

Wrens are not the neatest nest builders; their residences usually are cluttered with twigs gathered from here and there. But like some artists I know, the wren, with its soaring song and uplifting message of the morning, has its priorities straight. I am much more impressed with a beautiful song than I am with a carefully constructed nest.

Crows

Crows don't seem to appear on many people's lists of favorite birds. With their uniformly black coat of feathers, heavy, straight bill, short tail, and raucous call, they're not much like the friendly wren or the colorful bluebird or the entertaining catbird. On top of that, they're scavengers, not above robbing a songbird's nest and devouring any chicks they find there, and they seem to enjoy diving at the red-tailed hawks that soar over our pond on warm summer days.

Nevertheless, I have great respect for the crows on my farm. I admire the bird's willingness to tough out our northern winters. When I'm out for an early morning hike on a below-zero day, even if I see no other bird that winters here in the north—no chickadee, no blue jay, no nuthatch—I'll still hear a crow or see one flying overhead. Their piercing *caw, caw* may not be the most pleasing sound, but it's distinctive, and when I hear it I know I'm not alone. The crows, too, are stirring on this brittle Wisconsin day.

I rarely see just one crow, as they are social birds, dozens of them often gathering in one place. They also are highly intelligent. I remember as a boy going with my pa to visit an old-timer who lived alone on a little run-down farm west of Plainfield. The man had a pet crow living in his corncrib. He had taught the crow to say a raspy but understandable "hello." I developed an appreciation for crows on that day that has never waned.

Whip-poor-wills

When I was growing up, we usually heard the first whip-poor-wills in late May, after the grass had greened up, the oat crop was lush and growing, and the cornfields were ready for planting. Pa said the whip-poor-wills were calling *Plant your corn, plant your corn.* And it did sound like that as the seldom-seen night birds called over and over, sometimes a dozen or more times in a row.

At Roshara I've seen a whip-poor-will only a handful of times, but I hear them often. A medium-sized bird with a rounded head, dark eyes, a stout breast, and a long tail, the whip-poor-will blends in so well with leaf litter and tree bark that it's nearly impossible to see. These birds rest on the ground and fly up to capture moths and other insects that fly about in the evening.

In recent years I've heard them less often, and I've read that their numbers are in decline. But one of their favorite haunts happens be deciduous and deciduous-pine forests on sandy soil, which describes Roshara perfectly. I hope they will continue to thrive here, as spring without the call of the whip-poor-will just wouldn't be the same.

Barred owls

On a cool fall evening with no wind and the sky ablaze with starlight, from the northwest I hear the distinctive call of the barred owl: *Who cooks for you, who cooks for you-alllll?* The sound echoes through the still night and rolls across the pond valley. A few minutes later the call is returned. I've learned to mimic the call quite well, and I wonder what the owl who hears my call believes I am saying, especially when it answers me.

The barred owl is a large bird with a rounded head, big black eyes, and no ear tufts. Its brown and white plumage camouflages it well. Indeed, I've seen a barred owl only three or four times, usually sitting quietly on a lower tree limb and waiting for night, when it will hunt small animals silently, unnoticed.

Wild turkeys

Native to Wisconsin, wild turkeys were essentially wiped out here as settlers arrived, destroying much of the natural habitat and hunting them without regulation. The Department of Natural Resources reintroduced the birds to southwestern Wisconsin in 1976, and today wild turkeys can be found in every county in the state. I have a sizeable flock at Roshara. Without a fence they would raid my garden, but nevertheless I enjoy seeing them in all seasons of the year. On occasion I hunt them, but I have not been successful in bagging one.

Soon after the snow melts in spring and the sun feels a bit warmer, I begin hearing the *gobble, gobble* of a male turkey trying to impress a female. Occasionally I see a male displaying his long tail in a beautiful fan of feathers, competing with his fellow toms to impress one or more hens. The males of the species are larger than the females, and they have spurs (bony protrusions on the backs of the feet) and beards (hairy growth on the chest). The toms also are more colorful, with feathers in shades of bronze, gold, red, and green, while the hens are mostly a drab brown—better camouflage for them as they sit on their nests on the ground. By late spring the young turkeys appear, little balls of fluff, as many as ten or twelve of them hurrying after the hen. If they manage to escape predators, by fall they'll be nearly full grown.

Wild turkeys have excellent vision, especially in the daytime. They usually spot me before I see them. When I come upon a mature turkey, it takes off running on its long, strong legs, going as fast as twenty-five miles an hour. Occasionally, if I've surprised one, it will take off flying. They are powerful flyers, especially for short distances.

Surrounding one of our ponds are several huge old cottonwood trees, a favorite roosting place for our wild turkeys. Often just as it is getting dark I hear the turkeys flying up into the trees, where they will spend the night safe from coyotes and other predators.

Sandhill cranes

On a recent warm spring day, my grandson Ben was exploring along the shore of one of the ponds and got too close to a sandhill crane nest. The pair of cranes immediately began calling their loud, bugling rattle. Then one displayed the classic dropped-wing act, feigning injury to lure the intruder away from the nest. As we watched, they called again and again, their cries echoing through the valley. After Ben retreated, the sandhills calmed down.

For several years a pair of sandhill cranes has nested at our pond. They usually hatch two little ones in late April or May. And what beautiful birds they are. The adults stand up to four feet tall with a wingspan of five to six feet and are mostly gray, with red foreheads and long, dark beaks. But perhaps their most memorable characteristic is their call, a throaty, trumpeting, prehistoric sound that once heard is never forgotten. No other bird has a call like it.

According to wildlife biologists, in the 1930s sandhill crane numbers in Wisconsin had declined to about twenty-five breeding pairs due to hunting and loss of habitat. Today the sandhill population has dramatically increased, to the point that in 2012 a bill was introduced in the state legislature to establish a hunting season for sandhills.

We often see our pair at the pond. In the fall, when cranes congregate in hay fields and cornfields, we sometimes see dozens of them, all feeding together in preparation for their fall migration. In the spring sandhills are among the earliest to return to the north, sometimes arriving when there is still snow on the ground.

Big blue herons

My pa hated big blue herons—or shide pokes, as he called them. He believed that they caught more fish than any fisherman could ever hope to land. And if you saw shide pokes working along the shore in a lake where you were fishing—well, the fishing wasn't likely to amount to much.

I never said this to Pa, but I always liked watching big blue herons fish. And I believe I learned something from their fishing strategy. One time when Pa and I were fishing, I watched a big blue heron standing still for as long as three or four minutes without moving so much as a feather. Then, with lightninglike speed, it thrust its long beak into the water, impaling a fish. I was most impressed by its patience, its speed of attack, and its accuracy. I like to watch herons fishing at my pond; when one thrusts its beak into the water, it does not come up empty.

Both sandhill cranes and big blue herons have long, spindly legs, and both are seen wading in the water. One easy way to tell them apart is to look at them while they're flying overhead. Cranes fly with their necks outstretched, while herons fly with their necks tucked in. The big blue heron's call is dramatically different too, a kind of croaking sound that's not nearly as spectacular as the crane's echoing rattle.

Ruffed grouse

I've known ruffed grouse as long as I can remember. On the home farm, we had a good population of these beautiful little birds, which my pa called partridges. I see them at Roshara, though not as many: brown and grayish birds often sitting on the ground in wooded areas, so well camouflaged that unless they move, they are invisible. Both males and females display their tails in a fan of brown mottled feathers with an outer black band. Ruffed grouse have short, stubby wings that make an explosive noise when they take off, scaring the bejeebers out of whoever is close by. Those short wings allow them to turn sharply in flight, another good defense mechanism.

Most distinctive of all is the sound the male makes in the spring of the year during mating season: *boom... boom... boom;* then more quickly, *boom boom boom;* and then even more quickly until the booms are on top of each other and then disappear before the sequence starts all over again.

Along with the cry of Canada geese and the bugling of the sandhill cranes, the drumming of ruffed grouse adds to the chorus telling us that spring has arrived.

Changing Seasons

*To be interested in the changing seasons is a happier state
of mind than to be hopelessly in love with spring.*

GEORGE SANTAYANA

For those of us who live in the North, especially those who live on farms, the seasons dictate our lives. There is a time for planning and a time for planting, a time for harvesting and a time for resting, all determined by nature and its cycle of seasons.

As long as I can remember, I've looked forward to the cool, clear days of fall, when everything in nature seems a bit more relaxed as the frantic summer season winds down and there are still a couple of months before the temperature plummets and the snow flies. On the home farm, the harvest continued into fall as we brought in the corn, some for silage, some for cob corn for cattle, hog, and chicken feed. I remember the granary bins filled with oats, the corncribs overflowing with ears of corn, the haymows piled high with hay, and the silo filled to the top with corn silage.

Fall is still my favorite season, and when the colors splash across the woodlots—bright yellows, vivid reds, quiet browns—I never cease to be amazed, often turning to Ruth when I spot a maple tree that is especially colorful and saying, "Isn't that something?"

I find the sounds of autumn mysterious, haunting, even mythical: the call of Canada geese winging south from their summer home in the far north, the *rat-tat-tat* of a pileated woodpecker chiseling into a dead white pine, the barking of a gray squirrel from the top of a naked black oak, the call of an owl in the darkness on a quiet October evening and the call returned—a late-evening conversation between creatures of the night. Some evenings I hear the yapping of a pack of coyotes, *yip, yip, yip,* a sound that sends shudders up my back—though I don't know why, as coyotes are more afraid of me than I am of them.

These sounds make me think of the old Aermotor windmill on the home farm, how it squeaked and squawked on the dark nights around Halloween when the wind was up. In my upstairs bedroom I heard the noise and envisioned ghosts and goblins and creatures of the netherworld on their way to visit me.

Fall is my favorite season, to be sure, but still I look forward to the first snowflake drifting out of slate gray clouds, falling gently yet making a bold statement: fall is over and winter is here. Sometimes it comes in the night, quietly, without fanfare, little flakes at first and then larger ones, accumulating on the lawn, on the bare branches of the maple tree and the lilacs, and on the spruce tree that soon sags with the weight.

I don't dislike winter the way so many do. For me it has always been a special time, despite the inconveniences of dead car batteries, slippery roads, and the variety of other surprises it throws at us. When I was a youngster, that first snowfall told me that now the farm work would lessen and there would be time for reading, sledding, skating, and ice fishing, for hiking to the neighbors' for a visit, for pondering and planning for next year. Chores continued, of course, but there was more time to think and imagine and dream between keeping the woodstoves going and the chickens fed and the snow shoveled.

And then after a long winter came the joy of spring: flocks of geese flying north again in Vs that sometimes stretched from horizon to horizon, their calls breaking the silence of the morning and continuing long after sunset. The long-legged sandhill cranes returned too, their brash calls announcing their arrival.

At Roshara I know spring has come when the bluebirds return, the males with their sky blue backs and the color of the sun on their chests, the females more muted, looking for a nesting place in one of the many bluebird nesting boxes we have erected. The pond ice slowly melts, gray and honeycombed and sagging, and the wild mallards and wood ducks return, along with a pair of Canada geese that nests here every year. On a warm evening, the little spring peepers begin their song in unison as the sun sets. They continue all night long—sometimes so loudly that I can hear nothing but frog song as I stand at the pond's edge.

Spring also brings the wonderful sound of a ruffed grouse drumming—a series of ever-faster booms that to a farm boy sounds like an old John Deere tractor starting. Now I also see the wild turkey males strutting and displaying their many-feathered tails and gobbling their hearts out, trying to woo a female.

If fall is a rainbow of oranges, reds, and browns, the color of spring is green: light green of newly formed leaves, unfurling quietly but vividly as the days warm; dark green of grasses emerging from the tangled mass of last year's growth to capture the sun and announce that spring is here.

Spring is a time of promise and anticipation as we leave winter's challenges behind. Everything in nature seems happy, from the catbird singing its heart out at the top of the black willow windbreak to the newborn fawn bouncing along behind its mother on long, shaky legs. And there's nothing like the fresh smell of spring, especially after a rain shower.

Then suddenly summer is here, bringing heat, humidity, and mosquitoes. Everything is growing wildly, from the grasses to the newly sprouted oaks and aspen. The pines show their candles, this season's new growth. Bluebirds busily feed their young. Ducklings swim in a row behind their mother on the pond; a long-legged sandhill crane chick appears with its parents. A dozen goslings take swimming lessons while mom and pop keep a careful eye out for predators such as a pesky coyote looking for an easy meal.

In the evening, when the sun is sinking behind the woodlot to the west, I hear a whip-poor-will calling its name. I sit outside my cabin, resting, listening, and watching little brown bats swoop about in their relentless search for mosquitoes. (My woodshed is also a bat house where dozens of the creatures spend their daylight hours resting in preparation for another night of mosquito hunting.)

My memories of summer on the farm feature the cows heading out to green pasture, the lead cow's bell making its muted *dong, dong* as the cows graze, telling me where they are so I don't have to go looking for them in the night pasture.

In summer, thunderstorms boil up out of the west with flashing lightning and booming fury, dropping much-needed rain on parched crops. Everything grows rapidly: field and garden crops, grasses, trees, and, of course, weeds. The plants seem to be aware that now is the time to grow. It won't be long before fall comes and with it the first killing frost.

And so the seasons come and go, providing new experiences but also evoking memories of seasons past, reminding me how much the seasons influence what I do, when I do it, and even why I do it. And at a deeper level, the cycle of seasons reminds me that my life too follows a yearly cycle, of planning, hustling, and hurrying, and then resting, relaxing, and recharging before doing it all over again.

Life's Cycles

All my life's a circle;
Sunrise and sundown;
Moon rolls thru the nighttime;
Till the daybreak comes around.

HARRY CHAPIN

In nature there is a continual circle of birth, growth, decline, and death. For some creatures—certain insects, for instance—the cycle is complete in a matter of minutes. For a California redwood, it might last two thousand years. But even the redwood will eventually die. It is nature's way.

On a farm the circle of life is ever present. We saw the miracle of new life every year with the arrival of calves and piglets and kittens. And of course death came as well, sometimes planned, as when we butchered the animals we raised for food, and sometimes unexpected, when an animal died due to illness or accident or even occasionally for no reason we could determine. We celebrated the births and mourned the losses of those that died unexpectedly. And although it might seem unlikely that we would mourn the death of a hog that was destined to become meat on our table, sometimes we did that too. As a kid, I learned not to give names to the animals I knew were intended for butchering. Pa said it was a natural thing, just like harvesting potatoes and carrots and field corn. My mind agreed with Pa, but sometimes my heart didn't. I tried not to let him see that I felt bad when a favorite hog ended up on the dinner table. I had no qualms about killing a corn plant; butchering a hog was different.

Plants have a life cycle too, of course. As farmers we planted crops and garden plants with the intention that they would live and die within a single growing season, harvested as food for our table or sold to a food processor. For some harvested crops, such as oats and potatoes, and garden crops like squash, pumpkins, and sweet corn, we saved the seeds for planting the following season, so the cycle would be repeated.

The white oaks that grow at Roshara begin life as a tiny sprout emerging from an acorn. The fragile seedling struggles to compete with the surrounding grasses and plants for sunlight and moisture. Its life will end early if a hungry deer selects it for a tasty snack. But if the seedling grows, it becomes stronger and sturdier; soon it is a sapling that reaches my shoulder. It pushes out more branches, growing new leaves each season, capturing more of the sun's rays. The oak grows several feet a year, depending on rainfall, reaching a height at maturity of sixty or more feet and a diameter up to four feet. The tree might live for three hundred years if it is not struck by lightning or damaged by a windstorm or cut down by a logger. But it will not live forever. Yet even after death it might continue to stand in the woodlot, a leafless skeleton of a once majestic tree. Eventually it will fall to the ground and the wood will rot, slowly becoming a part of the earth from which it emerged. And even then, when its life cycle is complete, young oak saplings will grow nearby, some of them likely having sprouted from the acorns this old tree produced.

Just as the cycle of life is profound and never-ending, so is the cycle of day and night. Yet we tend to take sunrise and sunset for granted, especially if we have witnessed a goodly number of them. Some city dwellers rarely see the sun break the horizon in the east or sink in the west, blocked from view as they are by city structures. But it's not too difficult for people, no matter where they live, to find a place where they can observe sunrises and sunsets.

I remember rising before the sun on an early summer morning and trudging up the lane behind the barn to fetch the cows for the morning milking. Birdsong surrounded me, and dew hung heavy on the grass, the little beads of moisture reflecting the first rays of the sun as it climbed above the eastern horizon, a huge ball of yellow to welcome the day. I smelled the fresh-mown hay in the hay field I passed on my way, the rich aromas of drying sweet clover and alfalfa reminding me that today would be yet another day of making hay. On an old wooden fence post I spotted a meadowlark singing its song to welcome the day, filling the quiet of the misty morning with the sound of joy.

Just as spring is filled with hope and promise, so is the sunrise. My father often said, "Tomorrow will be a better day." As farmers we knew that no matter how difficult the previous day had been, the new day brought new opportunities.

If sunrise was a call to rise and greet whatever challenges and opportunities lay ahead, sunset reminded us to reflect on the day's accomplishments. Nearly every day, especially during the warm months, my father and brothers and I stood on a hill west of our barn and watched the sun set. We didn't say much, just stood and watched, each thinking our own thoughts as the sky turned orange and yellow and the sun slipped below the horizon, and then, as the light began to fade, the night birds began calling. Sunset was a time for reflection and assessment, for correction and planning. For Pa it was also a time to plan for the next day's weather. Simply by surveying the clouds at sunset, checking the direction of the wind, and testing the "feel" of the air, Pa could tell if rain was coming or if we would have another sunny day so we could cut more hay, or harvest more grain, or do whatever needed doing on the farm.

With each sunrise and sunset we moved forward, a day at a time, secure in Pa's certainty that the next day would be better.

Rain

Never curse the rain.

HERMAN APPS

Dry weather in central Wisconsin. Hot days, cool nights, no rain. Ten days ago the grass in front of my cabin was green, lush, and growing rapidly. This morning it is brown and crunches underfoot. The grass appears dead, but it's not. It is merely waiting for the next rain, when it will turn green once more. Tough stuff, this century-old grass that knows the ways of sandy, dry soils.

My garden suffers. Potato vines curl, squash leaves wilt, the bottom leaves of the sweet corn turn brown, and the tomato plants have stopped growing entirely. Even some of the weeds have wilted—but of course not all of them. Weeds know how to send their roots ever deeper, searching for life-sustaining moisture.

Those of us in central Wisconsin look to the western sky and wait for rain as farmers here have done for generations. These sandy soils never have enough rain. The rains in midsummer make all the difference, determining whether a crop will produce well, even survive. Farming sandy soil is a gamble—always has been, always will be.

We hope and pray for rain. Sometimes the rains come. Often they don't.

One of the earliest lessons I learned as a farm kid was to never complain about rain. No matter if it might spoil our plans, rain was always welcome. Without periodic rains on our sandy, droughty land, the cow pastures dried up, the corn crop withered, the hay crop wilted, and the vegetable garden suffered. No exaggeration: we needed rain to survive.

Rainy days were also days of rest. When the morning chores were done and the rain poured down, my brothers, Pa, and I would crawl up into the haymow and lie on the freshly stored hay, listening to the drum of the raindrops on the barn roof and smelling the sweet smell of clover and alfalfa hay. We might stay there for an hour or two, until Pa thought of some task that could be done while it rained, such as cleaning and organizing the pump house.

When the rain stopped or turned to a sprinkle, Pa might announce that it was a good day for fishing. My brothers and I would grab our long cane poles from under the eaves of the corncrib and dig up some earthworms in back of the hen house, and then we'd drive to Norwegian Lake, where we rented a leaky, wooden rowboat from the Andersons for a dollar (it didn't matter if you fished for an hour or all day, the rental price was the same). That evening we'd feast on fresh-caught bluegills accompanied by vegetables from Ma's garden.

In addition to all-day rains, we often had severe thunderstorms, especially on hot and humid summer days. They'd boil up out of the west, often in the early evening, and put on a show. As a kid I loved these storms, especially the wide-ranging display of lightning and the window-rattling thunder.

Many years later, when our kids and grandkids joined Ruth and me vacationing at a cabin on a northern Wisconsin lake, a grand storm rolled in from the northwest, growling and grumbling and flashing across the evening sky like Fourth of July fireworks. We sat inside watching the storm build over Lake George just east of Rhinelander. I have seen many thunderstorms over the years, and this one must have been seeking some kind of top-of-the-heap ranking. The sky darkened over the mirror-smooth surface of the lake; the thunder seemed to roll across the water, bouncing against the shore. The storm crept ever closer. Then the first raindrops fell, huge ones, the kind that strike the ground and send up a little splatter of mud in their wake. Looking out the cabin window, we watched the rain obscure the view of the cabin next door. The lightning flashes and thunder grew closer together. And then: a tremendous roar, a brilliant flash of light, a shower of sparks, and total darkness as the power went out. Lightning had struck a tall pine about fifty yards from the cabin, tearing a slice out of its top.

The grandkids had never experienced such a storm. They helped us light candles and find flashlights. Rather than being afraid, they saw the storm and the power outage as an adventure. We spent the evening telling stories by candlelight—and remembering that nature is a powerful force.

Wind

*If you wish to know the divine, feel the wind on your face
and the warm sun on your hand.*

THE BUDDHA

It's sometimes hard to believe that one of the most formidable forces in nature is invisible. We can feel the wind, and hear it, sometimes even smell it—or at least, we smell what it carries. But we can't see it.

My earliest memories of the wind and its sometimes devastating effects go back to the bone-dry years of the Great Depression, when the western sky over the home farm turned yellow as the westerly winds sweeping across the flat, sandy lands of old Glacial Lake Wisconsin lifted the soil into gigantic clouds. The dust, some of it as fine as talcum powder, sifted under the windows and gathered on the furniture, on the cupboards, on the kitchen stove, on everything. My mother despised the dust and the never-ending wind, but somehow she endured those miserable Dust Bowl days.

Wind made its power known on our farm again in early May 1950, killing several calves, injuring other animals, nearly toppling our barn, and turning our lives upside down. A fierce wind had been blowing all day: sixty, seventy, eighty miles an hour. Our oat crop was just coming up, and the wind tore up the oat seedlings and lifted the soil into the air. It smashed off tree branches, tore off barn and house shingles, and sent terror into the hearts of my brothers and me as we did our chores that afternoon. The wind howled all that day, unrelenting, and continued after sunset when normally the wind dies down. All night long it tore around the corners of my bedroom, an ominous, frightening sound. In the morning I awakened to pandemonium as my mother summoned neighbors with a general ring on our party line telephone, and I hurried to help Pa release the animals that were trapped in our barn, which was on the verge of tipping off its six-foot-high basement wall.

People from our neighborhood and beyond soon arrived to help. They managed to stabilize the barn and keep it from toppling, corralled the cattle in a safe place, built a temporary pen for the calves that had survived, tied the bull to a tree (he was as terrified as the other farm animals), and helped Frank and Charlie, our team of draft horses, from their stalls. All the while, the intense straight-line wind kept blowing, not a tornado but just as devastating. It was one of the most awful scenes I can remember from my growing-up years on the farm. The barn and the cows inside it were our main source of income, and all of it had nearly been destroyed. It would take several months of hard work to repair the barn so the animals, temporarily housed in a neighbor's barn, could return to the home farm. It was a trying time for both the animals and the family.

Wisconsin's winter winds are notorious too. At our farm the snow often came on strong winds that created drifts taller than me, plugged our country road, and made farm chores a challenge. A major snowstorm was usually followed by wind and bitter cold, with temperatures often well below zero. As one of our neighbors liked to say, "No matter what direction a north wind comes from, it always blows cold."

But like so much in nature, wind had its positive as well as negative effects. Wind turned our windmill, which pumped water for our animals and for family use. Wind dried the wash my mother hung on the clothesline north of the house. Wind dried the newly cut hay and the oats gathered into bundles and awaiting threshing day. On a hot July day, as the sun beat down on me while I hoed potatoes or cucumbers or green beans, a breeze made the job bearable. And awakening on a March morning to a breeze blowing in from the south, warm and refreshing and smelling like spring, was always welcome.

Farmers and other rural people know the importance of windbreaks to help protect farmsteads from storms and conserve precious soil. Pa planted a windbreak soon after he moved to the home farm in the 1920s, a row of red pines that stretched a few hundred yards, from south of the barn to the woodlot a few hundred yards north. The windbreak was designed to protect the farm buildings from the prevailing westerly winds, especially from the wicked thunderstorms that blew in from the west and southwest in summer and the frigid northwest winds that swept across central Wisconsin in winter.

At Roshara we have two windbreaks, one to protect the buildings and the other to stop soil erosion, both planted by previous owner John Coombes. Both continue to defend our farm from the battering winds. Unfortunately, on the level sandy lands to the west of my farm, where irrigation now provides the water necessary for bountiful crops of vegetables, many of the windbreaks planted during the dry years of the 1930s have been removed to allow the huge irrigation sweeps to move easily across these vast acreages. Wind erosion has again become a problem, especially in spring when the crops have just been planted and the land is open and susceptible to wind damage. Farmers here are once again experimenting with low-growing windbreaks that will allow the irrigation sweeps to move unencumbered but will also slow down the winds that tear at the soil.

The wind, so taken for granted by most of us—often not even noticed unless it happens to blow off our hat—is an integral part of nature. It plays many roles, some of them destructive but many of them beneficial. Invisible yet powerful, the wind demands our respect and our awe.

Winding Trails

Trails are the footprints of the ages.

JENS JENSEN

Ever since I was a little kid, I have enjoyed walking along trails. I spent untold hours, first with my pa and later on my own, trekking on the trails that wound through our woodlots, paralleled the old fence lines, and twisted across marshy areas where frogs and turtles and ducks offered sounds and sights that captivated me.

When Ruth and I bought a sixty-acre woodlot adjacent to our farm a few years ago, I discovered that it had no trails except those made by deer as they wandered through the property on their way to our two small ponds. Although the woodlot had once been logged, perhaps about thirty years ago, most of the logging roads had healed and were now nearly invisible. The remnants of one logging road remained, but it was crisscrossed by several downed trees and was not passable, even for hikers.

This woodlot was originally part of the acreage owned by Tom Stewart, who homesteaded this land; it was sold during the Depression years by the Coombes family so they could keep their one hundred acres of cropland intact. It has always been a woodlot, never cleared for farmland. The hills are extremely steep in places, and huge boulders are scattered about—likely exactly where they landed when the last glacier receded some ten thousand years ago.

The spring after we bought the woodlot land, Steve and I began planning a winding trail from our cabin to the far reaches of the property. It took us most of a week to decide where to locate the trail, as we carefully selected a path that would provide interesting scenery but require little cutting of trees or moving of boulders.

Clearing the trail became a family project. That April, daughter Sue and her husband, Paul, joined Steve and me, along with my brother Don, as we hacked out the trail in the woods. We started with chainsaws, handsaws, and brush trimmers, cutting through downed trees and slicing off low-hanging branches, working uphill and downhill between the two ponds, moving around stones as big as kitchen stoves and wading through blackberry thickets.

As we worked, I noted that trail building is a lot like life itself. We reach a high point and then suddenly are thrust into a valley. We face an obstacle and must decide if we should confront it or avoid it. We lob off the low branches of our life, and every so often—though not often enough—we stop for a moment to appreciate what we have done and enjoy the view.

When the trail was nearly complete, Steve and I climbed on my ATV to see if the path we had made was wide enough and if the little six-wheeler could climb the trail's couple of extremely steep hills. We headed down the old logging truck road, which connects to our new trail at the top of the first steep hill. After a couple of sharp turns, the trail drops down another steep hill and runs along the narrow spit of land separating our two ponds. Here the trail passes through a parklike area, with native grass and tall trees and expansive views of the ponds on either side. I turned off the ATV, and Steve and I sat and listened to the quiet broken only by the occasional sound of the wind high in the bare oak branches.

After a bit we moved on, up another steep hill, past giant black oaks and boulders the size of my farm tractor, up and up and up to what must be the highest point at Roshara, only a few hundred feet from my western boundary and three-quarters of a mile from the cabin. We stopped again and gazed off through the woods, still open and stark, as warm weather had not yet arrived to turn everything green. From there we had a wonderful view of the ponds at the bottom of the hill. Then we continued on where the new trail links up with the original farm trails. Soon we came to the prairie, five acres of open grassland, still brown and dormant. On we went, past my newly planted pine plantation, some seven thousand red pine trees only a couple of feet tall and waiting for the new growing season to send forth their candles of new growth. We stopped to look across the acres of pine and ponder what this view might be like in ten years, and then in twenty years.

We continued on the prairie trail that defines the south side of the farm and along a row of bluebird houses, where a pair of bluebirds had already staked out a nest box for the coming summer. We paused again to watch them busily building a nest. I made a mental note that several of the boxes had seen better days and needed replacing.

Now we lumbered along the old trail system that I had established forty years ago, heading down a steep hill alongside a slope where we planted red pines in the 1960s—trees now more than forty feet tall. Climbing another hill, we approached the white pine windbreak. Those old trees are the source of seeds that distributed over what was once a cornfield and has now become five acres of white pines, many of them nearly as tall as the mother windbreak pines to their west. The smell of pine permeated the air as we traveled farther east to the place where the lupines grow and the Karner blue butterflies thrive. The lupines weren't blooming yet, but in late May or early June a carpet of blue would appear here, along with the Karner blues.

At the lupine patch we turned north, following the trail through the white pines until we came upon an acre-size field that I keep mowed so deer can use it as a pasture and where I harvest grass each year to use as mulch for my garden. Traveling down one last small hill, we arrived at the cabin, having circled most of our 120 acres and feeling pleased with how our new trail added to Roshara's trail system.

When I am at the farm, I often follow my network of trails through the woods, across the prairie, along the flats and down the hills and around the many twists and turns that we purposely included. A trail is not for hurrying. Despite how familiar the trail is to me now, there is always something new to see or hear as I wind my way along. And there are the old friends: a deer bounding in front of me, the giant oak trees that I dearly love, the views across my ponds, where I often spot a mallard or a wood duck or a family of Canada geese. As the seasons change, the views from the trails change too, from the budding of the trees and the greening of the grass in spring to the rainbow of colors in fall to the naked maples in winter. Small side trails here and there lead to special views: a close-up look at the ponds; a trip to the prairie restoration. These two miles of trails provide access to a vast cross-section of central Wisconsin nature and landscapes, from upland forestland to wetlands to prairie. Traveling my farm's nature trails is one of the great joys of life at Roshara.

Pond Magic

While men believe in the infinite
some ponds will be thought to be bottomless.

HENRY DAVID THOREAU

We are lucky to have two ponds at Roshara, one entirely within our property boundaries and the second shared with a neighbor. They are kettle ponds, formed when the last glacier retreated and left behind huge blocks of ice that melted into small bodies of water. These ponds have no outlet or inlet. They don't have names, either; we merely refer to them as Pond I and Pond II. But they are part of a series of kettle ponds, starting with Chain O' Lake to the north of us and ending with Wagner's Lake a mile to the south, and are likely connected underground.

Our ponds actually are water table lakes, rising and falling with the region's water table. In the forty years we have owned Roshara, we have seen the ponds dramatically rise and fall twice. Pond I reached an all-time low in 2012, perhaps on average only three feet deep, but it has risen a bit since then. Still, it has a long way to go to return to the glory years of the 1980s, when it was filled to the brim and running over, forming a quarter-acre island on the west side and more than twenty feet deep in places.

Water use is a growing controversy here in Waushara County, especially use by farmers who install irrigation equipment and draw water from the aquifer. Critics of this growing practice point to nearby lakes that have completely dried up and streams that now flow only for brief periods.

The Coombes family, who worked this land before us, used Pond I as a source of water for their cows and hogs during times when water from the well was scarce or when there wasn't enough wind to power their well pump. Today the two ponds are sources of water and feed for untold numbers of birds and wild animals. They also provide nesting sites for sandhill cranes, Canada geese, and several species of ducks. Especially during the hot, dry days of high summer, the ponds provide a haven for wild creatures, from turkeys and deer to raccoons and songbirds.

For me the ponds are a source of untold enjoyment in all seasons. I often go to them simply to sit and listen and watch the goings-on of all the critters that live or visit there. In the spring of the year when the ice has just melted and the frogs are coming out of hibernation, I go to the pond in the early evening to listen to the spring peepers. These little frogs make a high-pitched peep similar to that of a young chicken, but much louder. I have been at the pond with Ruth when the peepers were so loud we couldn't hear each other talk. It's a mystery to me how these little frogs, also called chorus frogs, are able to sing so well together. I wonder which one is in charge of leading the chorus of celebratory spring singing.

On a hot midsummer day when the wind does not stir and the pond's surface is as flat as a floor, I go there in the evening to hear the call of the bullfrogs, a deep *harrumpf* somewhat like the lowing of a bull, a rumbling that seems the exact opposite of the spring peeper's high-pitched call. I even enjoy sitting near the pond in the rain, watching the raindrops collide with the water's surface and to create little whirlpools that form, spread, and disappear only to form again. The sound of raindrops falling on the pond's surface is a tinkling, almost bell-like sound, gentle yet impressive.

In fall I visit the ponds when the maples, aspen, oak, and birch that surround it are ablaze with color. I look for migrating ducks resting on their way south, and sometimes I am treated to the sight of a flock of Canada geese dropping out of the sky to spend the night there, eating and resting and feeling safe. One year I even saw a swan on the pond. It stayed for several days before continuing its journey to a warmer place.

When the ponds freeze and the leaves are down and there is a little snow on the ground, I stand at edge of the pond and watch the northwest wind play with the snow on its surface, making little swirls that form, disappear, and form again, nature as artist.

Roshara's ponds and surrounding marshland are a fascinating contrast to the oak woodlot, pine plantations, and prairie. Each of these unique environments provides homes to different plants, animals, and birds. Together they offer me a wide spectrum of life in the wild.

Wood, Fire, and Smoke

To poke a wood-fire is more solid enjoyment
than almost anything else in the world.

CHARLES DUDLEY WARNER

The old oak stood forty feet tall, a sentinel on the hill west of the cabin. The tree had died a couple years earlier, the bark falling from the upper branches, which now were bleached white from the summer sun. The oak remained sturdy and strong and now was a prime candidate for firewood to feed our ever-hungry woodstove.

Making wood has become a fall tradition at the cabin. The family gathers, and together we cut, split, and pile the wood against the woodshed to dry. The wood we'll burn this season was cut a year ago, dried for a winter and a summer and then stored in the woodshed. This well-seasoned firewood is both easier to light and safer to burn, with less danger of chimney fire.

My son Steve handles the chainsaw these days, and my son-in-law, Paul, is in charge of handling the cant hook, lifting the tree off the ground to help prevent the chainsaw from pinching. After Steve and Paul have the tree sawed into stove-length chunks, I haul the pieces to the shed near the cabin with the tractor, and there Steve and grandson Ben use an electric log splitter to slice the big chunks into woodstove-size pieces. Paul hauls the split wood with the tractor to the woodshed, where he and Steve's partner, Natasha, not only stack the wood but make the stack look like a piece of art.

Sue, Natasha, and Ruth prepare an enormous noon meal for the hungry wood-cutting crew. After a break for good food and a bit of rest, the work continues throughout the afternoon until all the wood from the tree we cut is split and stacked. I am reminded of the wood-cutting bees we had on the home farm when I was a kid, when the neighbors came to help, sometimes two or three times starting in the fall and often again in late March or April. In those days there were no chainsaws and no mechanical wood splitters, just two-man crosscut saws that Pa and I or sometimes a hired man used to cut down dead oaks. We cut them into lengths eight to ten feet long that we could haul with the team and sleigh or wagon to the farmstead, where they would await wood-sawing day. When the pile of logs and smaller branches was stacked high, the neighbors were invited to a wood-sawing bee to help cut the logs into stove-sized blocks that could be split with a splitting maul.

Guy York, a neighbor who owned a circle saw powered by an old Buick engine, did the actual sawing, as the neighbors carried the heavy logs to the machine and tossed the cut blocks onto a pile. A wood-sawing bee was a noisy, dirty, and difficult affair. The oak wood was heavy, usually wet with snow, and the circle saw screamed as it cut through the hard wood. But it was a task that had to be done, sometimes two or three times a winter if the weather was cold and winter days lingered on into April.

Following the wood-sawing bee, Pa and I split the big blocks into smaller pieces, ready to feed our woodstoves: two in the house, one in the pump house, and one in the potato cellar. Some of the smallest pieces would feed the tank heater, which kept the stock water tank from freezing on winter's coldest days.

Some of my earliest memories are of sitting by the wood-burning cookstove in our farm kitchen, watching my mother cook meals and bake bread and pies. Even with no thermometer to guide her, she knew just the right amount of wood to put in the stove for whatever she was preparing. When she lifted the lid to put in another stick of wood, a little puff of wood smoke would emerge, mixing with the mouthwatering smells of the food.

When I was out hiking on cold winter days, I always knew I was getting close to home or to a neighbor's place when I caught a whiff of smoke from a farmhouse chimney. Sometimes when I was walking home from school on a below-zero afternoon, I smelled wood smoke before I could see our buildings, and I knew I would soon be warm. The first thing I did when I got home on those frigid days was to crowd up to the cookstove, the warmest place in the house.

At age four or five, I was old enough to accompany my father ice fishing—an activity Pa dearly loved but one I found mighty uncomfortable on freezing-cold days. Once our tip-ups were in place, Pa and I would hike to the nearby shore. There we would gather twigs, dead oak leaves, and grass and start a smoky campfire. When the fish weren't biting—which was often—we huddled around the campfire, the smoke threading up through the trees and the orange flames providing a dash of color to an otherwise dreary day. Sometimes my uncles joined us, and as we huddled around the little fire they told stories of earlier days on the ice, of deer hunting, of close calls with nature—stories I never tired of hearing, illuminated by the light and warmth of the smoky campfire.

By the time I was around age ten, I loved reading about early explorers, and as I sat near our smoky little ice-fishing campfire I thought about those pioneers and what stories they shared as they huddled near their own. When I studied the cave dwellers, I pictured them gathered around a fire to cook their food and keep animals away, and I tried to imagine the campfire stories they must have told.

On winter days when I trekked to the woodlot with Pa to help him make wood, we would make a pile of dead branches, slowly adding to it as we worked. Later, when we paused in our work, Pa would set the brush pile afire and we'd huddle around it, watching and smelling the wood smoke as it trickled upward and dispersed into the cold sky. We marveled at the flames as they changed colors from yellow to orange to bluish as the oak twigs and leaves were consumed.

When I was in grade school, my schoolmates and I would sometimes gather on cold, clear nights for ice skating on Chain O' Lake, a mile and a half from our farm. On shore we'd build a campfire, a warm place to sit and put on our skates and to gather and talk. The smoke would drift across the lake, permeating our skating spot with that wonderful aroma so full of mystery.

These days I most enjoy a campfire when Steve and I take our annual canoe-camping trip to the Boundary Waters Canoe Area Wilderness of northern Minnesota. With the canoe pulled up on shore and our modest supper finished, we sit by our fire, listening to the sound of waves gently nudging the stones below our campsite and a lonely loon calling in the distance. I watch the smoke rise above the tree line and disappear, and I think about the voyageurs who traveled in these parts and who surely must have sat by a similar campfire at the end of their long day, watching the flames and listening to the loons. For me, the smell of wood smoke is a primitive smell rich with history and memory.

Being Neighborly

Every individual has a place to fill in the world and is important in some respect, whether he chooses to be so or not.

NATHANIEL HAWTHORNE

In our farm community, neighbors depended on each other. We came together to ease the burden of large tasks such as harvesting and putting up a new barn. And we hurried to one another's aid in emergencies, saving a house from a fire or taking turns doing chores for a farmer who had fallen ill. But we also looked to our neighbors for other things: a good story, a feeling of camaraderie, or even a new understanding of the world around us.

One of our most unusual neighbors was Morty Oliphant. His given name was Morton Calvin Oliphant, but we kids called him Morty Elephant—maybe because *Oliphant* sounded like *elephant,* or maybe because he couldn't pronounce his own name properly. Morty stuttered so badly you could scarcely understand a word he was trying to say.

A bachelor, Morty lived a couple miles south of us on a hilly, sandy, stony farm that he worked with horses. He had a ramshackle, never-painted house tucked against the side of a hill, a small barn behind the house, and a couple of outbuildings. Even after electricity came to our neighborhood, Morty lived with no electricity or indoor plumbing and used a woodstove to heat his house and cook his meals. He milked a few skinny Guernsey cows (his sole source of income), made a little hay, planted a garden, and lived a considerably more austere life than the one we lived a few miles up the road.

Most folks barely knew Morty Oliphant, though they talked about him plenty. My pa was one of the few neighbors who liked Morty and stopped by to see him. Pa most often paid Morty a visit in the winter, wanting to make sure he hadn't fallen or taken ill.

I remember the first time I accompanied Pa on one of those trips to Morty's place. I must have been four or five. It was a cold January day, the snow piled high everywhere. I could see a thread of smoke coming from the house's single chimney as we approached. We trudged up to Morty's kitchen door, and Pa knocked. Soon the door swung open, and I got my first up-close look at Morty Oliphant.

"Cuh...cuh...come in," he said in his halting way of speaking. To my surprise, Morty wasn't nearly as fearsome as people made him out to be. True, his white hair seemed to fly off in every direction, his beard was long and scraggly, and his bib overalls and flannel shirt were faded from many washings. But he was obviously pleased to see us on this cold winter afternoon.

"How are you, Morty?" Pa asked, shaking his hand.

"Pr...pr...pre...etty good," Morty stammered. He offered us chairs by the woodstove. Pa and Morty talked and

I listened, trying to understand what Morty was saying. Pa knew Morty well and was patient with him, waiting for him to say what he had to say, even though nearly every word was a struggle to get out.

After a few minutes Pa asked, "You still got that pet raccoon? I'll bet Jerry would like to see him."

Morty made a clicking noise with his mouth and, to my astonishment, a full-grown raccoon stepped out of a wooden box in a far corner of the kitchen. It walked to where Morty was sitting and looked up at him.

"Ha...ha...ha...ow are you?" Morty said to the furry animal. The raccoon cocked its head to one side and made a purring noise, not too different from the sounds I was used to hearing our barn cats make. Morty and the raccoon were clearly communicating.

Morty took an unshelled peanut from his pocket and handed it to the animal. The raccoon took the peanut in its paws, dropped it to the floor, and used its paws (almost like human hands) and its mouth to open the shell and eat the peanut.

"What do you think of that?" Pa asked me.

"It's really something!" I said. I had never seen a raccoon this close, and I had never seen one kept as a pet.

Morty offered the raccoon more peanuts, and soon there was quite a mess of peanut shells on the kitchen floor. With each peanut, Morty would say something I couldn't make out, and the raccoon would cock its head to the side and look right at him, making those purring sounds. After a bit, the raccoon walked back to its box in the corner. I sat there amazed at what I had just seen. But there was more to come.

"Does that other critter still live under your house?" Pa asked, smiling.

"Ya...ya...ya-up," Morty said as he got up from his chair. He bent over and lifted up a loose floorboard.

I was absolutely astounded to see a full-grown badger emerge from its home under Morty's kitchen floor. Pa had always told me that badgers were vicious and that I should avoid them. But this one calmly followed Morty over to his chair as Pa and I watched. Then Morty and the badger carried on a conversation—at least that's how it looked to me. I couldn't understand a word Morty was saying, but the badger could. And likewise Morty seemed to understand what the badger's quiet growls and purrs were all about.

After that day, I was always eager to join my pa on a visit to Morty Oliphant's place. I continued to be astonished by how this humble man, so often shunned by people because of his speech impediment, could relate to wild animals in a unique way. His animal friends didn't mind at all that he couldn't speak clearly. Those visits to Morty's farm stay with me still as examples of the importance of listening to the whispers and looking in the shadows for surprising insights into the natural world. I learned on those trips that some people have a special way with wild animals, and that we often can learn much from a neighbor.

Nature Writers and Conservationists

Those who dwell among the beauties and mysteries
of the earth are never alone or weary of life.

RACHEL CARSON

From my early experiences with our neighbor Morty Oliphant, I discovered I could learn about nature in many ways and from all kinds of people, even those who lived just down the road. When I reached school age, I began encountering other people who would have a profound influence on my personal philosophy about nature and wild places: the great nature writers and conservationists. Today I have a bookshelf packed with nature books on topics ranging from identification of wildflowers to what the natural world is likely to look like two or three generations from now.

For me few things are more meaningful than direct experiences in nature. But I've found that reading about nature and the environment enriches those experiences. It pushes me deeper into topics and provides a new perspective, another person's observations that I can compare with my own. On a fall day when the clouds hang heavy and a cold rain splashes against my cabin window, sitting by my woodstove with a book is about as good as it gets.

Horace Kephart (1862–1931)

I was first introduced to one of my all-time favorite books about nature and life in the wild when I was in eighth grade. I had just spent a week as a sort of hired hand for a new neighbor, George Luedtke, who had recently left Milwaukee with his family so he could raise his two sons in the country. He had bought my grandfather Witt's farm and taken up farming—or at least he was trying to. He had read every book about farming that he could get his hands on, but he quickly discovered that "book learning" does not prepare one for such practical tasks as milking a cow, harnessing a horse, plowing with a one-bottom plow, and a hundred other farming skills those of us growing up on farms knew and took for granted. George had bought a small herd of Guernsey cows and soon realized that he didn't know how to milk them. My father volunteered me to spend a week living with the Luedtkes, showing George how to milk cows by hand.

After a week of me doing his milking, George gave up and bought a milking machine. But to thank me for helping him, he gave me a copy of *Camping and Woodcraft* by Horace Kephart, a St. Louis librarian who later lived in the Great Smoky Mountains. From this clever guidebook, first published in 1906, I learned how to build a wilderness shelter and a campfire. I discovered how to make a drinking cup from a piece of birch bark. I learned about knots and edible plants. As I went about my chores twice a day at home, I passed the time dreaming that I was doing all those things Kephart wrote about.

I treasure my copy of *Camping and Woodcraft* to this day. I still look at it and dream, experiencing vicariously the outdoors adventures of Horace Kephart back in the early years of the twentieth century.

Carl Sandburg (1878–1967)

It was George Luedtke's father-in-law, Walter Stoesser, who introduced me to the poet Carl Sandburg. When I was in high school in the late 1940s, Mrs. Luedtke's mother and father came to live with them on their farm. Walter was in his late eighties, short, with white hair and a white mustache, well read—and highly opinionated. Walter was a walker, but not the kind of walkers that we were. Anytime we walked anywhere it was with a purpose or a destination in mind. But Walter Stoesser walked for exercise, which was a new idea for many people in our community. He walked around our country block—a distance of four miles—every day, timing himself and keeping detailed records.

While many folks in our community found Walter strange, I found him interesting, and I got to know him well. When he learned that I was interested in nature and in writing, he pulled a book off his impressive bookshelf and handed it to me: *Cornhuskers* by Carl Sandburg. I had encountered Sandburg's poems in my high school English classes, and I noticed that the poet's name was handwritten on the title page.

"Carl is a friend of mine," Walter said. He told me that Sandburg had once lived in Milwaukee. I had never met anyone who personally knew a famous author. Walter had every one of Sandburg's books, all personally inscribed to him.

I wasn't much for reading poetry, but I dug into the book and found Sandburg's writing melodic yet informative. Today I realize what a gift Walter Stoesser gave me. Who can forget a line so moving as this by Sandburg: "The prairie sings to me in the forenoon and I know in the night I rest easy in the prairie arms, on the prairie heart."

Henry David Thoreau (1817–1862)

One of my prized possessions is a copy of Henry David Thoreau's *Walden* that my children gave me when I completed graduate work at the University of Wisconsin–Madison in 1967. Susan was four years old and just learning to write her name, which is inscribed in the book; Steve was three and Jeff was two. I find myself rereading this book regularly, each time gaining new inspiration from this man considered by some to be our first nature writer.

Published in 1854, *Walden* isn't an easy read. Thoreau was a deep thinker and a keen observer of all things in nature, but in my estimation he was not a great writer. What I like about the book is that it's a very personal work, blending Thoreau's philosophies on life, politics, and nature. In it he recounts his experiment in living simply in a cabin on a sixty-two-acre pond, on land recently purchased by Thoreau's friend Ralph Waldo Emerson near Concord, Massachusetts.

Thoreau did not live, as some believe, as a hermit; he made regular trips to town, visited with friends at the cabin, and even gave lectures. He explained his decision to live in relative isolation in one of *Walden*'s most often-quoted passages: "I went to the woods because I wished to live deliberately, to front only the essential facts of life, and see if I could not learn what it had to teach, and not, when I came to die, discover that I had not lived."

Thoreau did not earn much acclaim in his lifetime; of the two thousand copies of *Walden* originally printed, some seven hundred unsold copies were returned to him. He died of tuberculosis in 1862 at the age of forty-four. But by the 1890s, interest in Thoreau and *Walden* began to grow.

For me, Thoreau is an example of someone who not only contemplated a different way of living, he pursued it. He understood what could be gained by a close association with nature, and he provided a foundation for the many nature writers who followed him.

John Muir (1838–1914)

It wasn't until I was attending the University of Wisconsin in Madison that I got to know the work of John Muir. One day as I was walking through the State Historical Society headquarters building on campus, I came upon a wooden contraption the likes of which I had never seen. It had skinny wooden legs and, most intriguing, hand-carved gears of a variety of sizes. The label attached said it was a "clockwork desk" built "by naturalist John Muir while at the University of Wisconsin, Madison, 1861–1863." Muir had designed the desk to perform a number of functions, including opening the book to be studied that day.

A classmate suggested that I read Muir's *The Story of My Boyhood and Youth,* and I was hooked. I enjoyed his descriptions of the tough times he experienced growing up in Marquette County, Wisconsin, and I marveled at his ingenuity, his resolve, and his drive to make a difference with his life.

Later I visited Muir's boyhood home on Fountain Lake, not far from Portage and only a brief drive from our farm in adjacent Waushara County. I stood at the edge of the lake and wondered if it was that view that had inspired a young Muir to become a great naturalist. He went on to be a champion of the wilderness, cofounding the Sierra Club in 1892 and lobbying for the expansion of the national forest system. He was largely responsible for the creation of Yosemite, Sequoia, Mount Rainier, and Grand Canyon National Parks.

Like all of the best nature writers, Muir captures readers' attention with details and vivid descriptions and then brings the reader into the story and creates an emotional response—even when writing about something as seemingly mundane as a pesky mosquito, as he did in *The Story of My Boyhood and Youth:* "The beautiful meadow lying warm in the spring sunshine, outspread between our lily-rimmed lake and the hill-slope that our shanty stood on, sent forth thirsty swarms of the little gray, speckledy, singing, stinging pests; and how tellingly they introduced themselves!"

Loren Eiseley (1907–1977)

I stumbled onto Loren Eiseley's writing when I was doing graduate work in the 1960s. The first book of his that I read was *The Immense Journey,* published in 1946, a collection of essays with their roots in Eiseley's home community of Lincoln, Nebraska. The book established Eiseley, a geologist and anthropologist by training, as a writer who could combine science and humanism in a compelling way. In *The Immense Journey* he wrote this about the coming of spring: "Every spring in the wet meadows and ditches I hear a little shrilling chorus which sounds for the world like an endlessly reiterated, 'We're here, we're here, we're here.' And so they are, as frogs of course. Confident little fellows. I suspect that to some greater ear than ours, man's optimistic pronouncements about his role and destiny may make a similar little ringing sound that travels a small way into the night."

Sigurd Olson (1899–1982)

Sigurd Olson, the son of a fundamentalist preacher, was born in Chicago and moved with his family to Sister Bay, Wisconsin, in 1906, when he was seven. His love for nature developed as he explored the woods, fields, and shorelines of Door County while avoiding his straitlaced, unapproachable father. The family moved to Prentice, Wisconsin, in 1909 and then to Ashland in 1912. Olson majored in agriculture at Northland College in Ashland and transferred to the University of Wisconsin in Madison in 1918. After graduating, he taught high school and college and began a writing career, penning articles for outdoors magazines. He eventually became dean of Ely Junior College in Ely, Minnesota, and worked as a canoe guide in the Boundary Waters during the summer months. He also became active in protecting the Boundary Waters from development and helped draft the Wilderness Act of 1964.

I met Sigurd Olson once, at a UW–Madison graduation ceremony in 1972, when I was teaching there and Olson was accepting an honorary degree. We had little time to talk, though I would have loved to have gotten to know this man referred to by biographer David Backes as "in many respects, a second John Muir." According to Backes, "Muir's theology, like Olson's, arose out of direct, joy- and wonder-filled experiences in nature, with subsequent reflection and reading giving form and adding nuances to those experiences."

Olson wrote several books, the most notable being *The Singing Wilderness,* published in 1956. In it he wrote: "The movement of a canoe is like a reed in the wind. Silence is a part of it, and the sounds of lapping water, birdsongs, and wind in the trees. It is a part of the medium through which it flows, the sky, the water, the shores. A man is part of his canoe and therefore part of all it knows."

Having canoed in the Boundary Waters Canoe Area Wilderness for more than thirty years, I can attest that reading Olson's writing about the area is almost—though not quite—as rich an experience as dipping my paddle in a Northwoods lake and allowing the canoe to drift like a reed as the wind gently pushes me along. For me Olson's ability to blend knowing with feeling, experience with emotion, establishes him as one of our greatest nature writers.

Gaylord Nelson (1916–2005)

Known both as a politician and as an environmentalist, Gaylord Nelson excelled in both categories. Born in Clear Lake, Wisconsin, Nelson graduated from the University of Wisconsin Law School in 1942, spent several years in the Wisconsin State Senate, and was governor of Wisconsin from 1959 to 1962. He was elected to the United States Senate in 1962 and served there until 1981.

Long interested in environmental concerns, in 1961 Nelson helped create the Outdoor Recreation Acquisition Program in Wisconsin, designed to expand state-protected parks and wetlands and financed by a one-cent tax on cigarettes. He was appointed to the US Senate Interior and Insular Affairs Committee, which allowed him to pursue his interests in the environment. He wrote bills to preserve the Appalachian Trail and to establish a national hiking trail system; sponsored and cosponsored bills to protect the St. Croix Wild and Scenic Riverway in Wisconsin and create the Apostle Islands National Lakeshore; and saw through the passage of the Wilderness Act and the Alaska Lands Act. Following Rachel Carson's publication of *Silent Spring*, Nelson introduced legislation to ban the pesticide DDT in 1965.

Gaylord Nelson is best remembered for founding Earth Day. I was lucky to be at the University of Wisconsin–Madison Stock Pavilion on April 11, 1970, when he introduced Earth Day to the large crowd gathered there. The audience was moved by his eloquent words. The same year, I asked Senator Nelson to write a foreword for my first book,

The Land Still Lives. In it he wrote, "Today, the crisis of the environment is the biggest challenge facing mankind. To meet it will call for reshaping our values, to put quality on a par with quantity as a goal of American life. It will require sweeping changes in our institutions, national standards for the goods we produce, a humanizing of our technology and close attention to the problem of our expanding population." His words are as important today as they were in 1970.

Aldo Leopold (1887–1948)

A Sand County Almanac tops the list of favorite books for many nature lovers. I became acquainted with the book in the mid-1950s, when I read a copy at Camp Upham Woods near Wisconsin Dells. At the time I did not know the book would become a classic.

The tragedy is that Leopold never saw the book in print, for he died on April 21, 1948, the year before it was published. The chair of the Department of Wildlife Management at UW–Madison, Leopold owned a sandy farm along the Wisconsin River in Sauk County that was the setting of *A Sand County Almanac.* He died of a heart attack while fighting a grass fire near the farm.

Born in Iowa and trained as a forester, Leopold spent his early career working for the US Forest Service in the southwestern United States. In 1924 he transferred to the US Forest Products Laboratory in Madison; nine years later he accepted an appointment as professor of game management in the University of Wisconsin's Department of Agricultural

Economics. In 1939 he helped organize what is now the Department of Forestry and Wildlife Ecology at UW–Madison.

An environmental visionary in many ways, Leopold crafted a land ethic that resonates with nature lovers throughout the world. In *A Sand County Almanac,* Leopold wrote: "When we see land as a community to which we belong, we may begin to use it with love and respect. ... That land is a community is a basic concept of ecology, but that land is to be loved and respected is an extension of ethics."

Storytelling

*A story is a way to say something that can't be said
any other way.*

FLANNERY O'CONNOR

When we stayed at Roshara when the kids were little, rather than read a story at bedtime, we created our own stories. The only rule was that the story had to somehow relate to nature and the farm.

The kids were snug in their PJs and sleeping bags in the cabin loft. The lights were out, the windows were open, and the only sound was the call of a whip-poor-will or some other night creature. I would ask each of the kids to select a character or two for that night's story. Then we'd talk for a bit about what should happen to these characters.

Here's an example of one of our bedtime stories that I later wrote about in my journal. It was a warm July night in 1970. At bedtime that evening, after the kids had spent the day playing around the pond, we settled in and began.

"What characters do you want in your story tonight?" I asked.

Sue replied, "I saw some ladybugs at the pond today. I want two ladybugs in the story."

Steve said, "I want a whale. Whales like water." Steve loved throwing in a character that would challenge the story-telling, and this evening was no exception.

Jeff chimed in, "I saw a caterpillar today. I'd like a caterpillar."

I asked what names the characters should have.

"Willie for the whale," said Steve.

"Lizzie and Lilly for the ladybugs," Sue suggested.

Jeff was thinking. "How about Karl?" He had a friend at school named Karl.

"Okay," I said. "What's the story?"

"Simple," said Sue. "A whale gets lost in a big rainstorm on the ocean, and when the rain stops, Willie the whale is in our pond."

No one questioned how a whale might end up in our little pond at Roshara.

"What next?" I asked.

"Well, that's easy," said Steve. "The ladybugs and the caterpillar want to talk to Willie. They've never seen a whale before, and they want to say hi to him."

Jeff piped up with a question. "How are they gonna do that? Ladybugs and caterpillars can't swim."

The loft was quiet for a bit. Then Sue said excitedly, "I know, I know! They'll float out to the whale on a big oak leaf."

"Okay," said Steve. "What if they float out to the middle of the pond and can't find the whale? What if the whale is under the water?"

Sue and Jeff pondered that circumstance.

"Here's what happens," said Sue. "They float out to the middle of the pond, and they can't see Willie anywhere. They end up on a little island in the middle of the pond. And you know what?"

"What?" asked Steve.

"The island is Willie's back. They've found Willie!"

"Wow!" said Jeff. "What next?"

"The ladybugs and the caterpillar tell Willie that they'll plan a big party to welcome him to the pond. They want Willie to feel at home in this strange pond so far away from his friends. And so that's what they did," said Sue.

It was quiet again in the loft, moonlight streaming through the window. I could tell by the looks on the kids' faces that they were captivated by the story they themselves had created. Soon all three were asleep, no doubt dreaming of ladybugs, caterpillars, and whales.

Every evening we concocted a new nature story, boldly mixing fantasy with reality. After a day spent exploring the physical world, the kids settled in to exercise their imaginations and creativity. They were learning about nature in a different way, and they loved it. They were also learning about storytelling and how much fun it can be. Many years later they still recall the stories we created in the cabin loft at bedtime.

Family Camping

Keep close to nature's heart . . . and break clear away, once in awhile, and climb a mountain or spend a week in the woods. Wash your spirit clean.

JOHN MUIR

Ruth and I first went camping with our kids in the mid-1960s, when the children were very young. For our first camping adventure, we chose a campground forty miles from home, so if something drastic happened, like the kids not wanting to spend the night in a tent, we could return home easily. The campground boasted a fishing pond, which added to its appeal.

We arrived at the campground late in the afternoon and unpacked our gear. I had purchased a Coleman camp stove and lantern, an aluminum cooking kit, and—for $27.50—a secondhand green umbrella tent, the kind with a steel frame, a wooden pole in the middle, and an extension in the back to accommodate an extra person. It had screened windows on the sides and back and a flap over the door that could be held up with two poles and ropes to make a little porch.

The kids and I set about putting up the tent while Ruth

unloaded the cooking equipment and food. The children had a grand time with the ropes and tent stakes and the idea of building a "house" out of canvas. After each child selected where to sleep in the rather tight quarters, we set off to the pond to try out their new fishing poles. I showed each of them how to thread a worm on a hook, how to toss the line into the water, and how to keep an eye on the little red-and-white bobbers.

"When the bobber goes under, lift up on the pole," I instructed.

Four-year-old Sue had her line in the water first and a big smile on her face, as she had mastered the art of tossing out her line with the first try. Three-year-old Steve was next; it took him a couple of tries, but then his bobber too was floating on the smooth surface of the pond. Jeff, just two at the time, had some trouble threading the squirmy worm on the hook but finally managed with a little help. He tossed his line into the pond with one try, no trouble at all.

Now all three bobbers floated in front of the kids. "I want to catch a big one," Sue proclaimed. She had been talking about fishing the entire drive to the campground. Soon there was a discussion among the three of them about who would catch the biggest fish.

Five minutes went by. Not so much as a nibble.

"When are the fish going to bite?" Jeff asked.

"You've got to be patient and quiet," I said. Young Jeff had little of the first and mostly avoided the second as he kept talking all the time.

A few more minutes went by, and the bobbers remained

motionless. I had walked the few steps back to our campsite to see if Ruth needed any help with supper. Then I heard it: a loud splash. I was sure one of the kids had either fallen in or hooked a big fish, and I hurried back to the pond. But no one had fallen in, and no fish had been caught. Jeff, in exasperation, had tossed his new fishing pole into the pond.

"That fishing pole is no good," he said as he marched past me on his way to the campsite with a very disgusted look on his face.

I waded into the pond and retrieved Jeff's pole, none the worse off for the dunking. Steve and Sue continued fishing, but they caught no fish that evening, big or little. After supper we sat by our campfire, watching the flames, roasting marshmallows, and listening to the frogs in the pond. Later we tucked the kids into their sleeping bags, and they went to sleep almost immediately. Any fears Ruth and I had had about the kids wanting to go home early were unfounded. It was clear they were thoroughly enjoying their first camping trip, even if the fish weren't biting.

That was just the beginning. We continued our camping adventures every summer until the kids were in high school and busy with summer jobs. We also spent many a summer weekend camping under the black willows at Roshara during the years we were making the cabin habitable. In 1976 I retired the badly worn tent and purchased a pop-up camper, the kind that folded into a trailer and could be pulled behind our car. Now during summer vacations we ventured farther from home. One year we drove to Florida with stops along the way, including a night in the Smoky Mountains.

We spent a couple of days in a campsite near Flagler Beach, where the children waded in the ocean, searched for seashells, and walked a nature trail through a marsh near the campground. Another year we motored east to Williamsburg, Jamestown, and Washington, DC. We stayed at campgrounds that offered hiking, swimming, and observing animals and landscapes we had never seen, always spending the nights in our tent trailer. We avoided RV parks, instead choosing state or county parks, which were quieter and more secluded and offered more opportunities to commune with nature.

One early morning near Yellowstone Lake in Yellowstone National Park, I woke at sunrise to a rustling sound outside the camper. I cracked open the door and there, not ten feet away, was an enormous cow moose. I quietly woke the family, and everyone got a look at the inquisitive creature. She wandered around the campsite for a few minutes and then disappeared into the deep woods. None of us ever forgot the experience.

We were camping near Yellowstone Lake at the beginning of the cutthroat trout season. Shortly after we arrived, we chatted with an old bearded fisherman who said we should try fishing in the lake. "I come here every year on opening day, and fishing is always good," he told us. He showed us a favorite lure, shining and golden, that he said always worked for cutthroat. I trekked over to the camp store and bought three of the same lures. I tied them on the kids' fishing lines, and we headed to the lake on a cool and misty mid-June morning.

Fishing regulations required that any fish longer than twelve inches be returned to the lake. I mentioned this to the kids, thinking to myself that with our luck we wouldn't have to worry about that rule. But I had brought my fish measuring tape just in case.

Steve tossed his lure into the lake and immediately hooked and landed an enormous thirteen-inch trout. We tossed it back. On their first casts, both Jeff and Sue followed suit, each catching a fish too large to keep. Patience was not necessary on this fishing outing, for on nearly every cast, a fish flopped up on shore. The three of them did manage to land enough smaller trout for a fish fry that afternoon.

Another day we followed the hiking trail to the top of Mount Washburn, elevation 10,243 feet and a three-mile hike from the trailhead. For the first mile or so we saw wildflowers we'd never seen before. A slight mist was falling when we started the hike, but as we got closer to the top the mist turned to light snow. It was a personal and immediate way for the children to learn how elevation can affect weather—something we couldn't experience firsthand at home. From the top of the mountain, through the light snow, we could see Yellowstone Lake, the Grand Tetons, and a panoramic view of northern Yellowstone National Park. What an adventure that day turned out to be.

Ruth and I found camping to be a wonderful way to teach our kids about the diversity and wonders of nature around the country and in our own backyard. At the same time, we all enjoyed campfires, family togetherness, sunsets in the

Rockies, sunrises over the Atlantic, and the quiet drumming of rain on the canvas roof of our tent camper as we snuggled in our sleeping bags and recalled the day's adventures.

Farther Afield

*The lovely places. The lonely places. The lost and forgotten
places. The places where we go to turn our back on the world,
the places where we go to get back into the world.*

JOHN A. MURRAY

One of the best places to learn about nature is at home—in
your own backyard, in nearby woods or fields or meadows,
in a neighborhood park. Indeed, I consider the farm where I
grew up and the land I care for now—with their varied landscapes, flora, and wild creatures—to be two of my greatest
teachers. But building on this foundation of knowledge, I've
found exploring farther afield to be a great benefit to my in-
depth study and appreciation of nature.

In my life I have been blessed to have access to several
special places where I can see, hear, smell, feel, and even
taste nature. These varied locations have made a difference
in my life, providing a never-ending array of new things to
see and opening my mind to new ways of thinking about nature's interrelatedness.

Boundary Waters Canoe Area Wilderness

For more than thirty years, Steve and I have canoed in
northern Minnesota's BWCAW, commonly known as the

Boundary Waters. A federally designated wilderness area within the Superior National Forest, the Boundary Waters is a quiet place: no background traffic noise, no cell phone service, no Internet, no radio, no TV. It is a land of birch trees and stately white pines, balsam fir and white cedar, moose and wolves and black bear and beaver, bald eagles, white-tailed deer, and pesky red squirrels that wait for campers' handouts.

In the Boundary Waters, loons are our companions— beautiful, large black-and-white water birds whose calls mystify and delight us. On a recent trip, a loon swam but a few yards off the portage from Hungry Jack Lake to Bearskin Lake as we put in our canoe. It looked us over and then called lustily to its mate somewhere in the distance. The return call echoed across the still waters of Bearskin Lake.

With no light pollution, clear nights in the Boundary Waters provide a sky filled with stars from horizon to horizon—and the opportunity to see satellites streaming across the sky, reminders of how today and yesterday are colliding in the night sky. If we are fortunate enough to be there when a thunderstorm brews in the west, we witness a lightning show that surpasses any Fourth of July fireworks celebration. Jagged flashes of lightning cut across the sky and thunder rolls across the lake where we are camped, and then we hear the wonderful sound of raindrops pattering on the canvas tent roof, a sound that takes me back to the home farm when I was a kid listening to raindrops on the barn roof.

For Steve and me, the Boundary Waters is special for just what it is: a place in the wild where we rest and restore; a place where stories are lived and shared.

Lake George, Rhinelander, Wisconsin

I first encountered Lake George in 1961, when I introduced my bride of less than six months to the "joys" of camping. Unfortunately, on our first night in camp at Lake George, it rained more than three inches.

Ten years later I began to teach writing at the School of the Arts in Rhinelander, and in 1972 Ruth and I returned to Lake George, this time with three kids in tow and enjoying the relative luxury of a rented cottage. Ruth and the kids canoed, boated, swam, and played in the sand while I taught.

More than forty years later, we still return to Lake George each year. Our group has grown to include our children, their spouses, as many as seven grandchildren, and even a great-grandchild. It's a great place for us to gather, especially now that our family is scattered from Wisconsin to Minnesota to Colorado.

Family brings us together, of course, but it is the place—the wonderful lake with its sandy beach, loons that call at night, wild ducks that circle the pier, and the occasional bluegill that allows itself to be caught by one of the grandkids—that makes this an unforgettable experience for the family each year.

Vail Valley, Colorado

My youngest son, Jeff, his wife, Sandy, and their kids, Christian, Nicholas, and Elizabeth, live in Avon, Colorado, in the Vail Valley. Their home backs up to a mountain and sits at an elevation of 7,500 feet.

My farm is scarcely above 1,000 feet high on top of its highest hill, and I am not especially fond of high elevations. It takes me a day or two to adjust to the elevation and accompanying thin air when we visit Jeff and his family. But they have lived in the mountains for more than twenty years, and I can see why they love it, with winter skiing, summer rafting, wonderful mountain bike trails, and the other mountain activities that are a part of their active lives.

A few years ago I helped them plant a vegetable garden, a challenge at an elevation with a short growing season between late spring frosts and fall snowfalls. But their garden grew and grew some more, and they harvested beans, lettuce, carrots, onions, and other vegetables. The bounty brought with it one challenge that I hadn't been expecting: the elk that came down the mountain in search of a vegetable morsel. (The barking of Cody, the family dog, provided a quick solution.)

The Rocky Mountains astound me. Though they can be difficult to drive through and, depending on the elevation, offer snowstorms in any month of the year, they are one of our country's most beautiful places. There is something about standing in a valley with mountains all around that helps us realize that we human beings, with all our fuss and fury and chest-pounding, are tiny, almost insignificant creatures. For me it's a humbling experience to visit the mountains.

Yukon Island, Alaska

For two summers in the 1990s, I was privileged to teach leadership development workshops on Yukon Island, in Kachemak Bay, off the tip of the Kenai Peninsula and south of Anchorage, Alaska. The only way to the island is by boat from Homer, so Ruth and I flew to Anchorage and caught a commuter plane to Homer, where we met Gretchen Abbot Bersch, whose family homesteaded Yukon Island in the 1950s. Gretchen, a professor of adult education at the University of Alaska–Anchorage, was my host for the workshop. As it turned out, she was also our boat driver, baker, cook, and all-around superior workshop administrator.

We traveled with Gretchen to her boat parked in a slip along the narrow, four-mile-long Homer Spit, and soon we were plowing through the waves on our way to Yukon Island. Nowhere have I seen such undisturbed natural beauty: water and mountains and spruce-covered islands. As we traveled, Gretchen told us about the students who would be attending the workshop, all of them part-time graduate students and full-time employees of everything from Alaska Social Services to the pipeline companies working the North Shore. I listened carefully, but I was also taking in the grandeur of the setting. The mountains came down to the water's edge, and the water was blue and clear.

We motored along for a half hour or so and then landed at a beach, unloaded our luggage, and trudged up a narrow, rocky path through the woods to the cabin where Ruth and I would sleep for the next several days. There was no indoor plumbing on the island and no electricity except for the solar panels that charged the two-way radio—the island's connection to the mainland. Water came from a long hose that had its source in a spring halfway up the mountain at the center of the island.

Just outside our cabin door I spotted an eagle's nest high in a spruce tree. We soon discovered that the eagles had little ones, for each time we walked under the tree, the eagles made a considerable fuss.

The workshops were held in early July, when the sun slips below the horizon sometime after 11 p.m. and rises again around 2:30 a.m. The twenty or so students camped in tents on the beach. They appeared to love every minute of it. We met in a partially constructed conference center looking out over the waters of the bay and the mountains in the background. Never have I seen such an inspiring view.

One afternoon, Gretchen's sister, a commercial fisher, arrived by boat and gave us several fresh-caught salmon. That evening the students built a fire of driftwood on the beach, and we feasted on salmon. The students fileted the salmon on the beach, and as we dined we watched several eagles feasting on the fish entrails.

Yukon Island, filled with beauty and immersed in nature, is a place for learning, but perhaps just as important it is a place for recharging one's batteries and reconnecting to a simple way of living.

The Clearing Folk School, Ellison Bay, Wisconsin

Jens Jensen, a noted landscape architect who emigrated from Denmark and later lived and worked in Chicago, bought this property high on the bluffs above the waters of Green Bay as a summer home in 1919. He moved there in 1935 and founded The Clearing as a retreat center where "city people" would renew their connections to the land. Jensen believed that our environment has a profound effect on us and that an understanding of one's "place" is fundamental to clear thinking—a philosophy reflected in the name The Clearing.

I have taught writing classes at The Clearing since 1991. Few places offer such a wonderful opportunity to be immersed in nature while having access to skilled teachers in a variety of subjects. What I appreciate most about The Clearing is its focus on slowing down, getting in touch with one's self, and experiencing nature directly, with few intrusions from the outside world. There are no TVs, and cell phones are to be used only in designated places. The sleeping accommodations are log and stone cabins. Meals are taken together in a comfortable dining room that looks out over the bay. Often in the evening students gather around the council ring overlooking the bay and, as the campfire crackles in front of them, quietly watch the sun set. It is a wonderful place to unwind, to think, and to write without the intrusions of the outside world.

Keeping a Nature Journal

Journals allow one to reflect, to step outside oneself.

ALEXANDRA JOHNSON

I began writing in a journal when I was twelve years old. I was recovering from polio and had been confined to bed for many weeks. My Aunt Louise often stopped by with a new book for me to read. But on this day, Aunt Louise held in her hand a little diary.

"I thought you might like to jot down each day's happenings," she said.

I didn't want to tell her how I really felt: that each day was like the one before it and that nothing, absolutely nothing, was happening. My bedroom felt like a prison cell. My right leg was frozen. I couldn't walk. But it was late winter, and the weather was changing. The snow was finally melting; I could see some green grass out my bedroom window. So I wrote down what the weather was like each day as that winter finally gave up and spring began showing its face.

I have kept a nature journal pretty consistently ever since. I always start with a note about the day's temperature and weather. I write many other things as well, many of them about life at Roshara. I describe what's happening at the ponds, the oak woods, the prairie, the garden, the pine plantation, and the lupine patch. I keep a separate journal for my annual trips to the Boundary Waters with Steve; there I describe campfires and loon calls, sunsets and thunderstorms, bears and moose and quiet.

I often include a story, a deeper and more detailed description of something I've seen or done or something I'm thinking about. As a writer, I find my journal a good place not just to record my experiences in nature but also to explore deeper themes and try out ideas for future writing projects. I wrote this in my journal in January a few years ago:

Some things to do in the New Year:

Start a journal and write in it every day or even once a week. Record the weather. Pen your thoughts. Write a story from your past. Remove an emotional ache from your system.

Take time to see the whiteness of fresh-fallen snow that sparkles and glimmers and covers the grime and dirt of an earlier day.

Watch the sun set when the temperature is below freezing and the sky is steel blue and turns black as the sun sinks away and the temperature plummets.

Listen for the silence of winter, when snow buries the land and the cold tightens its grip. There is great beauty in silence, something that is in short supply these days.

Stand in a snowstorm and watch snowflakes accumulate on your sleeve. Each snowflake is different, each one special—a reminder of nature's creative magnificence.

Sit by a fireplace or a woodstove doing nothing except listening to the occasional pop of the fire and smelling the hint of wood smoke that sneaks into the room.

Remember that doing nothing is sometimes the most important thing you can do.

Anyone can keep a nature journal, no matter if you live in the country or the city. Jot down a note about a bird you saw on the way to work or a wildflower you spotted growing next to a roadway. Describe a summer thunderstorm or the antics of a squirrel at a birdfeeder. A journal is a personal thing; you don't have to worry about writing style, sentence structure, or punctuation. Sometimes you'll want to write just a phrase or even a single word. Or you may want to go beyond observations and write about your deeper philosophies and values concerning the natural world. All are grist for a journal. A nature journal can also include more than writing. Include a sketch of a robin's nest or attach a photograph cut from a magazine or newspaper. Copy down a quotation from a nature book that you especially love.

Journaling is a wonderful activity for children. Encourage the kids in your life to write down their observations of the natural world at home, around their school, or near the soccer field. Keeping a journal reminds children that nature is all around them.

Writing in my journal has become an essential part of my life, and I enjoy doing it with pen and paper. Often something mystical occurs when ideas generated in my mind flow through a pen and become visible on paper. Sometimes I'm really not fully aware of the idea—the depth of it or the intensity of my feelings associated with it—until I write it down.

There are other ways to keep a journal, however. You might want to transition from a completely private diary to a more public, online journal where you can share your observations and photographs with others. I write a weekly blog that people can sign up to receive by email or follow on Facebook or Twitter.

Journaling is an excellent way to explore the various dimensions of our philosophies and values about nature. The process of writing can help clarify and even uncover our deepest beliefs and values.

A Personal Nature Philosophy

Look deep into nature, and then you will
understand everything better.

ALBERT EINSTEIN

Each of us has an abundance of beliefs and values related
to nature. Together they comprise our philosophy of nature. We have held some of these beliefs since we were
children, and very often they are buried so deep within
us that we are not aware of them. Yet they influence our
understanding of nature and our sense of its value in our
lives.

My father never spoke of values, but I learned about
his values every day as I watched him and worked beside
him. Many of those values became mine. From my father I
learned the importance of rotating crops to allow the land
to recover and rejuvenate. I learned the importance of re-
storing nutrients to the soil, which Pa did by applying manure from our cows, horses, hogs, and chickens. I learned
how vital it is to conserve soil by watching Pa plant windbreaks and leave steep hillsides unplowed.

I also learned that land is much more than a place where
a living can be made—although that was extremely im-

portant to us as farmers. My father taught me that land is something that can be loved, must be respected and revered, and ultimately is in short supply. He never used any of those words, but through his actions he taught me what to value about land.

Yet while our personal philosophy of nature is foundational to how we think and act, it is also dynamic, always subject to change. As time passes and circumstances change, we respond to the evolving phases of our lives, to new experiences, and to new knowledge by revising our values and beliefs.

My mother cared for a flock of laying hens, usually about a hundred of them. Their eggs were a source of food for our family, and my mother sold the extra eggs and used the money to buy groceries and birthday and Christmas presents. She was proud and protective of her flock and considered any animal that might steal a chicken—weasel, fox, or hawk—the enemy. Thus I grew up believing that any critter that might raid the chicken house should be shot on sight, no matter where I might see it. In fact, when one of us saw a "chicken hawk"—usually a red-tailed hawk—soaring over the farm, we usually took a shot at it. If we killed one, we fastened it to a fence post near the chicken house to dissuade other hawks from stealing chickens.

I held these beliefs for many years, not bothering to consider their validity. But as I learned more about hawks (and more about chickens, too), my beliefs began changing. Through my studies I discovered that not all hawks are "chicken hawks." I learned that hawks have an important place in nature and are not automatically an enemy to be shot on sight.

Some elements of my philosophy of nature have remained the same since I was a child—the importance of caring for the land, appreciating the beauty of the changing seasons, respect for wildlife, enjoying a sunset, growing a garden. But in other ways my thinking has evolved. I continue to enjoy fishing, but I do little hunting. I enjoy watching a squirrel or a rabbit or a Canada goose more than I do shooting one. Today I hunt deer more to carry on a family tradition than out of the thrill of the hunt or the need to put food on my table.

Throughout my life I have continually rediscovered and revised my personal nature philosophy through my formal education and reading, through my writing projects, and perhaps most important through my experiences on my farm. And I've come to believe that without nature, civilization as we know it will not survive. My nature philosophy reflects deeply held values that I want to preserve, try to follow diligently, and strive to share with others.

Always Learning

Nature teaches more than she preaches.

JOHN BURROUGHS

No matter how well I come to know nature and the environment, there is always more to learn. In fact, seldom a day goes by that I don't learn something new. Every year my prairie restoration project teaches me, presenting me with a wildflower I've never seen before, a wild grass that I can't identify, or a bird's song I don't recognize. The more time I spend at my pond, the more I realize how little I know about pond life with its many plants and creatures, some of them visible, some under the surface. Every new experience intrigues me and challenges me to dig out my guidebooks and do more studying.

At the same time, and especially in more recent years, I find myself continually searching for deeper meanings, trying to figure out how plant and animal species relate to one another, the effects of seasonal changes, the ways wet and dry weather influence plant and animal populations. As I try to understand climate change, I look for the effects of longer growing seasons and warmer winters on the plants and animals at my farm. Beyond simply identifying what's around me, I'm continually looking in the shadows and listening to the whispers, searching for meaning, and trying to anticipate what the future of nature will be.

As I understand more and know nature more deeply, my personal philosophy also evolves. My continual learning leads me to take action: from writing about the natural world and supporting nature groups to caring for the forest at Roshara, taking steps to restore our prairie, and encouraging lupines to grow so the endangered Karner blue butterfly will continue to flourish here.

As a parent and longtime teacher, I have tried to pass on my knowledge, beliefs, and values about nature to my students, my children, and my grandchildren. When I was a kid, the *process* of learning about nature was as important as the things I learned. Keeping that in mind, I try to do fun things outdoors with my kids and grandkids. Some of the best photos in my vast collection of grandkid pictures are those of the youngsters grinning ear to ear while holding up the fish they just landed. While they're having a great time fishing, they are learning not only about patience—an important virtue when fishing—but also about where and how fish live, what they eat, and what eats them. On a day spent fishing, the kids will see fish (if we're lucky), but they'll also spot pond lilies, cattails, ducks, redwing blackbirds, a turtle or two, frogs, maybe a sandhill crane, a big blue heron, and more. Throughout the experience they are listening and watching and learning without even being aware of it.

Planting and maintaining a vegetable garden is another excellent way of introducing children to nature. Steve and

Sue and their families share a large vegetable garden at Roshara with Ruth and me. We all contribute to the planting, weeding, and harvesting, and we all take home our share of fresh green beans, potatoes, sweet corn, tomatoes, and much more. In the process we all benefit from the experience of working in the garden and nurture a close tie to the land.

Being a gardener also ensures my continued education in the ways of the natural world. Every year as a gardener brings surprises, successes and failures, and lessons to be incorporated into next year's gardening experience. I read garden books and magazines, attend gardening expos, and chat with other gardeners about what they do and how they do it. I'm especially interested in caring for our garden soil so that it not only produces a reasonable garden crop but also is improved year by year.

For young people, belonging to clubs such as the Boy Scouts, Girl Scouts, 4-H, and Future Farmers of America is another great way to experience nature directly. My grandsons in Colorado are active in the Boy Scouts and have gone on camping trips in all seasons of the year. While they're learning to identify wildflowers and wild animals and gathering the skills for wilderness survival, they're having a great time and learning to value nature. But even kids who don't have access to these kinds of organized groups will have opportunities to learn about nature in their elementary, high school, and college classrooms. Courses in earth science, chemistry, and biology provide a foundation for nature learning; studies in ecology, geology, geography, meteorology, and environmental sociology add to this foundation.

We're never too old to learn, and adults can enroll in classes and workshops about geology, soil conservation, wildflower identification, climate change, and a host of other topics to enhance their understanding of nature. If you'd rather get outside of the classroom, nature tours and trips are available in nearly every part of the world, from birding tours to glacier hikes to wilderness canoeing. And much can be learned by visiting local, state, and national parks, many of which have naturalists on staff, ready to explain the history and unique features of their surroundings.

Few things are more satisfying than learning something new. And with its many mysteries and complexities, nature offers learning opportunities and adventures to last a lifetime.

Slowing Down and Disconnecting

Nature does not hurry, yet everything is accomplished.

LAO TZU

I learned the importance of slowing down from my father. Pa said there are times when you should hurry, like when rain threatens a load of hay, but more often, he said, slowing down and taking things as they come is the way to do it.

Yet as the years have passed and the world seems to have sped up, I've often had to remind myself of his words—*slow down, be patient, take your time, what's your hurry?* Nature is not in a hurry, but we humans are. We want our gadgets to work faster, our travel time shortened, our meals prepared in minutes. Fast is good; slow is bad. Carl Honore said it well in his book *In Praise of Slowness:* "In this media drenched, data-rich, channel-surfing, computer-gaming age, we have lost the art of doing nothing, of shutting out the background noise and distractions, of slowing down and simply being alone with our thoughts."

We speed down a country road, and when asked what we saw on the trip we reply, "Oh, nothing." We are so interested in the destination that the trip itself has come to mean nothing—it's merely an annoyance, something to contend with as we hurry to whatever end point we have in mind.

To appreciate nature, to come to know it better, I know I must slow down, even stop on occasion. Next I must remind myself to keep relearning how to see, hear, smell, taste, and feel. I must constantly rediscover the use of all five senses. Watch a two-year-old in a grassy field on a summer day. The little one doesn't merely look at a piece of grass but tastes it, smells it, moves it around with little fingers to feel it. As children we naturally use all our senses. But as the years pass, we rely more and more on just seeing and hearing—and sometimes those fail us as well. Using all of our senses is necessary to truly know nature. And as my father so often reminded me, looking in the shadows and listening for the whispers requires that I hone *all* of my senses.

I once wrote about an old black willow that stands at the end of the windbreak at my farm. When my editor read the passage, he told me, "You really don't know that tree very well. See if you can become better acquainted."

I was taken aback, for I had walked under that old tree for many years, watched it as the seasons changed, marveled at its tenacity to withstand the windstorms that blow in from the west. But my editor was right. I had only a superficial knowledge of the tree, a "hurry-up, pass-by-quickly" kind of knowledge. So I endeavored to get acquainted with the old willow. I sat under it for hours on end. I listened to the wind play with its leaves on a breezy day; I felt its rugged gray bark. I tasted a bitter twig. I looked at its gnarly limbs sticking out this way and that, many of them cracked and bent and twisted by the relentless wind. I tried to picture what the tree had witnessed since it was planted in 1912. The more I got to know the old willow, the more I appreciated it and imagined the wonderful stories it had to share.

My editor was pleased with my work. I was too, and I had relearned a valuable lesson that my father had taught me: how to sit quietly in the woods, listening, watching, smelling, waiting patiently. Many times Pa and I walked into the woodlot behind our farmhouse on a cool fall Sunday afternoon and at first saw only trees and shrubs, no animals or birds. As we sat quietly, not talking, not moving, animals began appearing; first a squirrel, then another, high up in a tree in front of us. A chickadee perched on a nearby shrub, calling its cheery *chick-a-dee, chick-a-dee.* I wondered where these creatures had been hiding, and I wanted to ask—but I knew better, for silence still ruled. Then I saw a crow high up in a tree not far from us and to my delight, high above the trees, a flock of Canada geese flying in their long V.

Today, when I am caught with a multitude of projects that demand my attention, with deadlines that loom and pressure that mounts, I escape to my farm, slow down, and allow my senses to connect me to the nature that is all around me.

Research shows the value of being alone in nature, undisturbed, especially for overstressed people. As writer John McKinney explained in an article titled "Thoreau Was Right: Nature Hones the Mind," "The more worries (particularly about work and money) an individual had, the higher the typical level of restoration experience, and the more reported benefits gained from getting out into nature." McKinney goes on to explain that "nature engages your attention in a relaxed fashion—leaves rustling, patterns of clouds, sunsets, a bird, the shape of an old tree. Nature captures our attention in subtle, bottom-up ways and allows our top-down attention abilities a chance to regenerate." Of course, this "attention restoration theory" has been described in other terms by Henry David Thoreau, John Muir, and many other nature writers through the years.

For me, the value of being alone in nature is more than a merely restorative experience. It is a *connecting* experience, a reminder that I am part of something that is much larger than I am. It is a truly spiritual experience.

At the same time, these moments of solitude surrounded by the natural world allow me to *disconnect* from the bustle of the everyday. Most people these days insist on being connected at all times, either through some electronic gadget or in person. For these "hyperconnected" people, the idea of being alone is unnerving and, with today's technology, unnecessary and unwanted. Indeed, I have known people to experience a kind of "connectedness withdrawal" when I suggest they unplug and disconnect.

Some years ago Steve brought his friend Rick along on our annual canoe-camping trip to the Boundary Waters. Steve noticed that Rick was about to pack his Sony Walkman and headphones in the canoe along with our tents, cooking equipment, and other provisions.

"No Walkman," said Steve.

"Why?" asked Rick incredulously.

"We're going into the wilderness," answered Steve.

The Walkman was left behind. On the third day of the trip, I spotted Rick sitting alone on a rock near our campsite, looking out over a pristine lake with no human habitation in sight, nothing but the lake and the trees and the quiet sound of water lapping on the rocks. I didn't disturb him, but the look on his face said it all. It was a look of utter contentment and peace. Experiencing solitude can do that for a person.

Every month of the year, I spend several days alone at Roshara. We have no landline telephone there, no television. I go to the farm to find solitude, to get away from the bustle of my everyday life with its many interruptions and challenges. There I can come out from behind myself and look around and reevaluate my life and my work. I might retreat to the depths of my oak woods and merely sit, doing nothing, listening to the sounds of nature all around and experiencing peace. Or I might sit on top of the hill that looks out over my prairie, where there is nothing but clouds and sky and the quiet sound of the wind moving through the grasses. There I am able to return to a feeling I had when I was a child, a feeling of having room to stretch my arms without interfering with another person, a feeling of being a small part of something much larger than I was, and I marvel at the idea.

Listening to the Land

Come, listen to the earth with us. For those who have learned
to hear its song, the earth can soothe the troubled heart,
refresh the weary, soften the hardened, redirect the lost.

STEVE VAN MATRE

In our *hurry, hurry* lives, the idea of taking time to listen to
the land sounds not only a bit strange and impossible, but
also like a task easily set aside in favor of demands deemed
more important. Yet listening to the land might be one of
the most important things we'll do in our lives, whether we
make our living from the land or simply want to continue
having a ready supply of food on our tables.

Land is much more than an inert bit of soil upon which
we can erect a building, create a parking lot, or even grow
some leaf lettuce in a backyard garden. It is alive, filled with
organisms of every shape and kind.

Like other living creatures, land has a history. Unfortunately, the history of land in North America is a tale of
abuse and misuse. Pioneer farmers did not know how to
keep soil healthy and well supplied with nutrients or how to
prevent soil erosion. When the land was depleted, many of

these farmers moved on to locations where the soil had not yet been plowed and eroded, and they repeated the process. The land has a way of sharing its history, if we take time to listen. On my farm, the history of abuse nearly shouts. The huge gulleys torn into several of the hillsides describe the dramatic soil erosion caused by plowing up and down the steep hills. The mound of soil that stretches for a quarter mile along the white pine windbreak tells of the soil erosion that occurred here in the 1930s, before farmers understood the importance of windbreaks.

Most Native American societies considered the land to be Mother Earth, something to be revered and tended for the next generation. The concept of individual ownership of land was introduced to this continent by the European settlers, who, upon wresting the land from the Native Americans through a long series of one-sided treaties, immediately surveyed and divided it into parcels intended for individual ownership.

To be sure, the early settlers prized land ownership. And there is nothing inherently wrong with owning land—indeed, it can be a very good thing when the owners choose to respect and nurture it. But along with land ownership emerged the belief that a person could do whatever he or she wanted with that land. Land quickly became a commodity—a means of production existing solely for its potential income. There were exceptions, of course, and some farmers made a living from their land while also caring for it. Those who didn't, however, caused damage that even today is not fully repaired.

With the agricultural revolution that followed World War II, farmers replaced draft horses with tractors and replaced lanterns with electricity, and agriculture began changing even more dramatically. Starting in the late 1950s, technical innovations—from huge farm implements to genetically modified crop varieties—led to farms becoming larger and the number of farmers shrinking to a low of about 1 percent of the population today. As farms got bigger, tractors more powerful, and agricultural technology more pervasive, the use of land as a commodity only grew. Even as big farmers and agribusinesses took care to return nutrients to the soil—sometimes in the form of manure from mega-dairy or hog operations—they did so in the interest of increasing yields and creating profits. Money over reverence.

But there is a spiritual dimension to the land. Native Americans referred to the deeper meanings in nature when they talked about the four directions. During a workshop I taught at the University of Manitoba in Winnipeg, participants were exploring their personal philosophies of education and sharing their fundamental beliefs and values. One of the students, a Native American, described how the power of the four directions guided his life: sun, air, water, and earth. "South represents the sun," he began. "North represents the earth, east the air, and west, water." He went on to explain how the philosophy of the four directions was taught to him by his father, who had been taught by his father. "It has been a way for generations of my family to recognize the importance of nature and our tie to it," he told us.

Along with clean water and clean air, the land is the foundation for humankind's future on this planet. And the land, like all living creatures, wants to be respected, honored, and valued. It tries to tell us this, if only we'll learn to listen.

Last Hunt

Do the best you can with what you've got.

HERMAN APPS

My father enjoyed fishing and hunting his entire life. Born on a farm in 1899 and a lifelong farmer himself, Pa hunted and fished both for enjoyment and out of necessity, as these activities put much-needed meat on the table. Hunting and fishing were also ways he communed with nature, experienced it directly and deeply. We fished together in summer and winter from the time I was four years old and could scarcely hold up a cane pole. And as soon as I was twelve years old and could buy a hunting license, we hunted together.

Pa kept fishing and hunting even after he turned ninety. But in the summer of 1992 he wasn't feeling well. He didn't complain—it wasn't his way—but I could tell by observing little things that his health was deteriorating. By that time I was doing his bookkeeping for him, writing checks and making sure his finances were in order. When I told him he could save money on a magazine subscription renewal by taking the two-year offer, he replied, "Better make it just one year."

That summer we went fishing a couple of times, but I could see that his shortness of breath had taken some of the fun out of catching big catfish in Pony Creek. On his ninety-second birthday, in September of that year, I mentioned the deer hunting season that would begin in November. "I'll go if I'm up to it," he said.

My brothers and I had wondered if Pa should sit out the hunt that year, resting at home where it was warm and comfortable and he didn't have to do any walking. But he would have none of that talk. Deer season is a tradition. You don't let it pass by unless you are on your deathbed.

The next couple of months graced us with pleasantly warm days, cool nights, and no mosquitoes or other pests to annoy us as we hiked in the woods. The oaks, maples, and aspens slowly turned to many shades of brown, red, and yellow. The colors were as vivid as I remember ever seeing, and the leaves stayed on longer than usual, with few heavy, driving rains to blow them off the trees.

I drove Pa out to Roshara several times that fall, often after visting my mother, who now lived in a nursing home. Pa would walk a little in the yard, poking here and there with the cane he now carried. He no longer invited me to walk with him down the trail to the pond, something we had done many times over the years. I knew that the hill from the pond back to the buildings was just too much for his heart.

So I drove him down to the pond in my truck. He sat on the seat next to me, looking out over the water. Not saying anything for a moment, just looking. Then he began to speak. "Remember when that buck deer—big one he was, ten points at least—jumped in the pond and swarm across? Damnedest thing. Don't see a deer doin' that very often. Usually they'll run along the edge. But not that old buck. Nobody got a shot at him, either. He climbed out of the water and shook himself like a big dog. Too far away for a shot by then." A smile spread across Pa's heavily wrinkled face, which still had traces of tan from his many years of farming and tramping in the outdoors.

We got out of the truck and looked for deer sign around the pond, tracks where they had come to drink, places where bucks had rubbed velvet from their antlers on the aspen trees. A ruffed grouse jumped up in front of us. "Should have brought along the shotgun," Pa said. "Have us some partridge for dinner."

"Wonder how the ducks are doin' this year," he said, looking out over the pond. "Sure would like to have me some duck. Heck of a better thing to have on your plate than a tame turkey. Turkey meat's too dry. No flavor to it. Now you take wild duck, the way Ma used to fix it . . . " I could see a flood of memories returning to him as he recalled the days when my mother was well and cooked wild game of every kind—rabbit, squirrel, pheasant, duck, goose, venison—whatever Pa brought home. He didn't finish that last thought, just stood quietly, his thoughts likely with my mother at the nursing home.

As we stood side by side in the bright sun pouring down from a deep blue, cloudless sky, I could hear his labored breathing, a kind of a wheeze that I knew had been getting progressively worse the last few months.

"I remember when my brother, Fred, and I hunted ducks on these ponds," Pa said. In the early 1900s, Pa's family had lived on a poor sandy farm only a mile or so west of where we stood. "One time Fred and I snuck down to the pond just west of this one. It was a foggy day and everything was quiet and still and you couldn't see a thing. Could hardly see to the end of a gun barrel. Fred had his old 10-gauge shotgun—a beast of a gun, heavy as carryin' a lead pipe. And kick! Why, that thing sent your shoulder into spasms. Like an old plow horse let loose with a hind leg and hit you square in the shoulder."

Pa was smiling now, and his breathing seemed to come easier as he recalled the tale. "Well, me and Fred, we kind of hunkered down and eased toward the pond, tryin' not to make a sound. As we got closer, we heard a noise—sounded like a flock of chickens working in a chicken yard. But it wasn't chickens, it was ducks. And it sounded like a lot of 'em.

"Well, before you knew it, there was the pond, right in front of us. There in the mist were all those ducks. Mallards, I think they were. A bunch of shadows floatin' on the water. Then the whole damn flock just took right off at once, quacking away like you can't imagine.

"I says, 'Fred, shoot! Shoot!' *Kaboom.* The sound of that 10-gauge just about knocked me over. But that was nothing like the pain Fred was feelin' from that old shotgun slamming into his shoulder."

Pa paused to catch his breath. I asked if Fred had killed any ducks that day.

"Killed any ducks? Why, there was ducks fallin' out of the

134

sky all around us. It was rainin' down ducks. We must have gathered up a half dozen. There's few hunters that can get six ducks with one shot. But Fred did. And it's the truth, too." The biggest smile I'd seen in a long while spread across Pa's face.

I knew that Pa must be thinking about deer hunting. Telling that hunting story surely got him pondering the hunt coming up in November. Would he head out to the woods with us again?

That October I was helping Pa harvest his garden, saving the roots from the giant dahlias, digging the last of the onions and potatoes, gathering up the pumpkins and squash and carrying them to the root cellar in his basement. Pa stood by, telling me how to do what I had been doing for fifty years. He gave me instructions the same way he did when I was eight years old. I had never developed gardening skills that quite met his standards, and he still chided me to do better, to be more careful with the digging fork, to shake the dahlia roots just so. "You want to shake off some of the dirt, but not all. Leave on some dirt, and they won't dry out so much," he explained.

"It'll be deer hunting season soon," I said, hoping to get some indication of his intentions this year.

"Yup. Gotta buy my license, oil my rifle, and see how many bullets I got."

There was my answer. He was planning another hunt.

"This year I think I'll just sit down by the pond and see what comes by. Good place to watch for deer down there, you know."

"Yes, it is," I said.

"Yup, if somebody chases the deer out of Cain's woods, they have to come right by the pond. Or if they come runnin' from the south they'll come right by the pond too. Good place."

"It is," I agreed.

The night before the start of hunting season, Steve, Ruth, and I gathered at Pa's house to discuss opening day, something we had done for many years. My brother Don, his three sons, and Steve's friend Rick would join us the following morning at Roshara. I told Pa I'd be back in the morning to pick him up.

A half hour or so before daylight, I drove to Pa's place, and there he was, waiting. He was dressed in his Sorrel boots and faded orange jacket and cap; his deer rifle in its shabby case lay on his lap.

"Got your bullets?" I asked.

"Yup."

"Got your hunting knife?"

"Yup. Got everything I need. Better get goin' so I can be on my stand before daylight."

When we arrived at Roshara, I asked, "Need a ride down to your stand?"

"Nope. I can make it."

He shuffled off into the dark without his cane, down the trail toward the pond. In the crook of his arm he cradled his .30-30 lever-action Savage deer rifle with open sights, as he had every year since he bought it in the 1940s.

By late morning, when the hunters had gotten cold and

started to move around, Pa wandered south of his stand and came upon Steve and Rick. They were standing on the edge of our white pine windbreak, looking out toward the big field to the west. Steve carried his .30-30 Winchester with a scope; Rick had a .30-06 Remington. The three were quietly talking when Rick said, "Look at that."

A buck and two does bounded across the field two hundred yards away. Rick and Steve both began shooting, missing every shot.

"Which one's the buck?" Pa asked excitedly.

"The last one," Steve said.

Pa pulled up his Savage and fired.

Crack! Crack! The buck fell and didn't move.

Steve and Rick glanced over at Pa. He lowered his rifle and smiled. He didn't say anything, but he had a "there's how you do it" kind of look on his face.

My father was ninety-two years old, shooting a rifle that was nearly as old as he was. He had killed a running deer with two shots through the neck, with open sights, at a measured distance of 240 yards. Steve and Rick still scratch their heads about that day. There they were, in their thirties, hunting with scopes, and they hadn't touched the buck.

That was Pa's last hunt. His health steadily declined, and he died the next July. The following deer season saw only two generations of hunters in our woods.

During that 1993 season, as I walked around the pond, alongside the white pine windbreak, and across the big field where Pa killed his last buck, I sometimes thought I heard his voice on the wind and felt his presence beside me. He had hunted for more than eighty years and enjoyed every minute—the warm, beautiful days of fall when the sky is never more clear and blue, the cold winds and snowy days of early winter, and through it all the fun of being outdoors with sons and grandsons.

Now, twenty years later, I continue to hunt deer with my son, my brother, and my nephews every fall on my farm. Recently my grandsons Christian and Nick have joined the hunt. As we gather and tell hunting stories, the story of the year Grandpa Apps downed a buck with an open-sight rifle still tops the list. He instilled in all of us a love of walking in the woods on a cool fall day, listening, watching, hoping for a chance at a ten-point buck. I'll never forget what it was like when Pa was with me, showing me the way, helping me see what appreciating nature meant by doing it rather than merely talking about it.

Suggested Reading

Apps, Jerry. *Old Farm: A History.* Madison: Wisconsin Historical Society Press, 2012.

Apps, Jerry. *The Travels of Increase Joseph.* Madison: University of Wisconsin Press, 2010.

Berry, Thomas. *The Great Work.* New York: Random House, 1999.

Berry, Wendell. *Life Is a Miracle.* Washington, DC: Counterpoint, 2000.

Berry, Wendell. *The Unsettling of America.* New York: Avon Books, 1977.

Bjornerud, Marcia. *Reading the Rocks.* New York: Basic Books, 2005.

Carson, Rachel. *Silent Spring.* New York: Houghton Mifflin, 1961.

Eiseley, Loren. *The Invisible Pyramid.* New York: Charles Scribner's Sons, 1970.

Eiseley, Loren. *The Star Thrower.* New York: Harcourt Brace Jovanovich, 1978.

Emerson, Ralph Waldo. *Nature and Other Writings.* Edited by Peter Turner. Boston: Shambhala, 2003.

Fox, Michael. *One Earth One Mind.* New York: Coward, McCann & Geoghegan, 1980.

Freyfogle, Eric T. *The New Agrarianism.* Washington, DC: Island Press, 2001.

Goodenough, Ursula. *The Sacred Depths of Nature.* New York: Oxford University Press, 1998.

Gore, Al. *The Future: Six Drivers of Global Change.* New York: Random House, 2013.

Haskell, David George. *The Forest Unseen.* New York: Penguin, 2012.

Honore, Carl. *In Praise of Slowness.* New York: HarperCollins, 2004.

Jensen, Jens. *Siftings.* Baltimore: Johns Hopkins University Press, 1990.

Kingsolver, Barbara. *Small Wonder.* New York: HarperCollins, 2002.

Leopold, Aldo. *A Sand County Almanac.* New York: Oxford Press, 1949.

Logsdon, Gene. *A Sanctuary of Trees.* White River Junction, VT: Chelsea Green Publishing, 2012.

Louv, Richard. *Last Child in the Woods.* Chapel Hill, NC: Algonquin Books, 2005.

McKibben, Bill, ed. *American Earth.* New York: The Library of America, 2008.

McKibben, Bill. *The End of Nature.* 1989. Reprint, New York: Random House, 2006.

McKibben, Bill. *Enough: Staying Human in an Engineered Age.* New York: Henry Holt, 2003.

Muir, John. *The Story of My Boyhood and Youth.* Madison: University of Wisconsin Press, 1965.

Murray, John A. *The Quotable Nature Lover.* New York: Lyons Press, 1999.

Olson, Sigurd F. *Listening Point.* 1958. Reprint, Minneapolis: University of Minnesota Press, 1986.

Olson, Sigurd F. *The Singing Wilderness.* 1956. Reprint, Minneapolis: University of Minnesota Press, 1984.

Rutstrum, Calvin. *The Wilderness Life.* Minneapolis: University of Minnesota Press, 1975.

Salwey, Kenny. *Muskrat for Supper.* Golden, CO: Fulcrum Publishing, 2012.

Suzuki, David. *The Sacred Balance.* 1997. Reprint, Vancouver, BC: Greystone Books, 2002.

Thoreau, Henry David. *The Bluebird Carried the Sky on His Back.* New York: Stanyan Books, 1970.

Thoreau, Henry David. *Walden.* Boston: Ticknor and Fields, 1854.

Tishler, William H., ed. *Jens Jensen: Writings Inspired by Nature.* Madison: Wisconsin Historical Society Press, 2012.

Van Matre, Steve, and Bill Weiler. *The Earth Speaks.* Greenville, WV: The Institute for Earth Education, 1983, 1994.

Wirzba, Norman. *The Essential Agrarian Reader.* Lexington: The University Press of Kentucky, 2003.

Acknowledgments

Many people contributed to this nature memoir.

In my early years growing up on the farm, my father, Herman Apps, taught me about nature and instilled in me a great love for it. He was a farmer with limited formal education, but he knew the names of trees and their growing characteristics, the names of wild animals and their traits, the ways of the weather and an appreciation for it, and much more.

I owe a large debt of gratitude to Howard and Joan Sanstadt, both of whom worked for the *Waushara Argus* in Wautoma in the 1960s. When Howard agreed to publish my column "Nature Notebook" starting in 1966, he launched my professional writing career.

Many others have helped and encouraged me. Heading that list are my wife, Ruth; sons, Steve and Jeff; daughter, Sue; Sue's husband, Paul; and Steve's partner, Natasha. A special thanks to my grandchildren for their interest in nature and for their probing questions: "What is this?" "How does this happen?" "Why is this important?"

The folks at the Wisconsin Historical Society Press, especially press director Kathy Borkowski and marketing manager Kristin Gilpatrick, deserve my unending gratitude for their support, encouragement, and assistance. A very special thank you to Kate Thompson, senior editor at the Wisconsin Historical Society Press, for her hard work in making my sometimes scattered thinking coherent and my tangled syntax readable.

There are many more who have helped me along the way. A big thank you to all.

About the Author

STEVE APPS

Jerry Apps has worked as a rural historian and environmental writer for forty-eight years. For ten years he wrote a weekly column on nature appreciation for several central Wisconsin newspapers. He has written many books on nature and environmental topics, including *The Land Still Lives; Cabin in the Country; Old Farm: A History; Campfires and Loon Calls;* and *Garden Wisdom.* In 2012, Wisconsin Public Television produced the hour-long documentary *A Farm Story with Jerry Apps,* which included many of his beliefs and values about nature and the environment. He and his wife, Ruth, divide their time between their home in Madison and their farm, Roshara, near Wild Rose.